NORTH CAROLINA'S HURRICANE HISTORY

JAY BARNES

The University of North Carolina Press

Chapel Hill & London

NORTH CAROLINA'S
HURRICANE
HISTORY

The paper in this book meets
the guidelines for permanence
and durability of the Commit-
tee on Production Guidelines
for Book Longevity of the
Council on Library Resources.

Library of Congress
Cataloging-in-Publication Data
Barnes, Jay.
North Carolina's hurricane
history / Jay Barnes.
     p.   cm.
Includes bibliographical
references and index.
ISBN 0-8078-2201-9 (alk. paper).
—ISBN 0-8078-4507-8
(pbk. : alk. paper)
     1. Hurricanes—North
Carolina—History.   I. Title.
QC945.B37   1995   94-30638
363.3'492—dc20   CIP

99 98 97 96 95   5 4 3 2 1

Design by April Leidig-Higgins
Graphics by Jackie Johnson

Title page: The awesome fury of hurricane Hazel is evident in this photo by Hugh Morton, taken near the peak of the storm at Carolina Beach. Morton and several other reporters witnessed the destruction, including *Charlotte News* staffer Julian Scheer, seen here struggling against the rising tide. This photo won Morton first place in spot news in the 1955 Southern Photographer of the Year competition. (From *Making a Difference in North Carolina*, by Ed Rankin and Hugh Morton; photo courtesy of Hugh Morton)

Page v: The people of North Carolina have always managed to show great spirit in coping with the turmoil caused by major hurricanes. (Photo courtesy of Roy Hardee)

Page vii: Wrightsville Beach Yacht Club after hurricane Hazel, October 1954. (Photo courtesy of the N.C. Division of Archives and History)

Page ix: A young girl wades through the streets of Carolina Beach after the passing of hurricane Hazel in October 1954. (Photo courtesy of Hugh Morton)

*This book is dedicated
to the many North
Carolinians whose
lives have been lost
to hurricanes*

*and to my father,
James T. Barnes Sr.*

CONTENTS

NORTH CAROLINA'S HURRICANE HISTORY

INTRODUCTION

Hurricanes. They brew themselves out of the heat of the tropics, spinning blindly across the open sea. Often they evolve into massive storms with violent winds and torrential rains. They may live for days or for weeks, and most die off harmlessly as they wander over cooler waters. Some cause widespread alarm by tracking unpredictably close to land. But occasionally, these storms become deadly intruders as they strike our coastlines with random fury. Hurricanes, and their counterparts around the globe, are the greatest storms on earth, killing more people worldwide than all other storms combined.

We plot their growth, give them names, and track their movements across the sea. With each hurricane season, we wonder if *this* will be the year of *the* storm. The vast majority of North Carolina residents have never experienced a severe hurricane, knowing only the frightening video reports of distant tragedies like Andrew in 1992 or the faded news clippings about the great storms of the 1950s. But North Carolina has had a long and brutal hurricane history. Countless big storms have overwashed our coast and battered our state, and many North Carolinians have lost their lives in the desperate struggle against water and wind.

Some still recall the great storms, like Hazel, and tell amazing accounts of the destruction they caused, and more recently, hurricane Hugo rocked the Carolinas, creating a modern disaster of epic proportions. But few stories are told of the other severe storms that have swept through North Carolina. This collection of photographs and words pieces together that history and may provide some insight into the nature of our hurricane threat.

Isolated barrier islands and broad, shallow sounds are the dominant features of the North Carolina coast. The barrier islands, including those that make up the Outer Banks, offer the mainland some protection from hurricanes and winter storms. These islands line the extensive coastline, stretching over three hundred miles from Calabash to Corolla. Through the years, hurricanes have reshaped the coast by moving massive amounts of water and sand, overwashing the barrier islands, and opening and closing inlets.

Today these coastal islands support thousands of homes and businesses and have become major tourist destinations. Growth in the coastal zone continues at a rapid pace, bringing more and more people near the ocean. In ever-increasing numbers, residents and vacationers strive to be close to the water, where they can enjoy bright, sandy beaches and the smell of salt in the air. However, many have built in areas that may suffer from the advances of a major hurricane. To most, that threat is vaguely understood as an acceptable risk.

Hurricanes that strike North Carolina usually have their greatest impact

Automobile accidents are common during hurricanes, as residents rush to seek shelter from advancing storms. During hurricane Ione in 1955, a portion of Highway 24 washed away, causing several cars to crash and claiming one life. (Photo courtesy of Tony Seamon)

along the coast. Rising storm tides and large waves inundate low-lying areas, sometimes flooding streets and homes and sinking boats. Most of those who have lost their lives to these storms have been trapped by rapidly rising water.

But the devastating effects of a hurricane are not found only along the shore. Large, powerful storms, like Hazel and Hugo, create widespread destruction as they track inland and can bring chaos to metropolitan areas like Raleigh and Charlotte. Gusting winds can uproot large trees, snap utility poles, and cause extensive property damage hundreds of miles from the ocean. Torrential rains fall as these massive storms weaken over land, creating flash floods that can affect several states. Powerful storms striking the Gulf states, like Camille in 1969, have even been known to track northeast, causing devastating flooding throughout the Appalachian Mountains.

Through the years, all parts of North Carolina have been battered by hurricanes. Until Hugo swept a path from Charleston, South Carolina, through Charlotte in 1989, North Carolinians had seen three decades of relatively few hurricane strikes. Although moderate storms had made landfall, like Diana in 1984 and Gloria in 1985, there had been few powerful midcoast hurricanes in the sixties, seventies, and eighties. Hurricane Donna struck Carteret County in September 1960 and was the only *major* hurricane to make a direct hit on the North Carolina coast during this period. Hurricane Emily came extremely close to landfall on the Outer Banks in 1993, close enough to cause significant destruction at Cape Hatteras. But in the 1950s, eastern North Carolina became known as "hurricane alley," as six hurricanes hit the state within seven years. In fact, hurricanes Hazel, Connie, Diane, and Ione all made landfall within a twelve-month period, from October 1954 to September 1955.

Prior to the 1950s, hurricanes were rarely given names, and most can only be recalled by the dates of their occurrences. North Carolina was struck by other severe hurricanes in this century, including memorable storms in 1944, 1933, 1916, and 1913. Records of hurricanes from long ago are somewhat less complete than those of more recent storms, and photos of hurricane events from the nineteenth century are rare. Notable hurricanes from the 1800s occurred in 1899, 1883, 1879, 1856, 1846, and 1837. Many other significant storms hit the state in previous centuries, although even fewer details of these storms' effects are available.

Early newspaper accounts of hurricanes were often delayed for days, as communications were disrupted and travel was difficult after the storms. Firsthand accounts of storm damage from the remote Outer Banks sometimes never reached the major newspapers of the Piedmont, although those journals often ran lengthy reports of hurricane destruction in Florida, Charleston, Norfolk, and New York. Few photographs of North Carolina hurricanes were taken prior to the 1940s, largely due to the scarcity of cameras in the mostly rural coastal communities. Fortunately, weather stations in various statewide locations kept accurate records of wind speeds, rainfall, and the barometric pressures by which these storms are measured.

This history of North Carolina's hurricanes was compiled from a wide variety of sources, including newspaper reports, historical publications, letters, National Weather Service records, and personal interviews. In some cases, stories of coastal residents and their hurricane adventures have been passed along like other down-east folklore and offer amazing accounts of destruction and survival. Photographs that illustrate the impact hurricanes have had in North Carolina are historical treasures. Those contained in these pages were collected from museums, newspapers, libraries, government agencies, businesses, and family albums.

Many individuals provided valuable assistance in building this collection of photographs and events. It may be of greatest interest as a photographic journal and record of a great state with a stormy past. But hopefully, by improving our understanding of these uncommon weather events and their local effects, we can better prepare and know what to expect when the next major hurricane strikes the North Carolina coast.

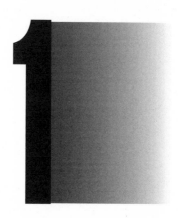

BIRTH OF A HURRICANE

*Hurricane Diana approaches
the North Carolina coast in 1984,
as seen from a weather satellite.
(Photos courtesy of the National
Weather Service)*

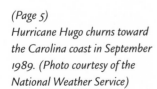

*(Page 5)
Hurricane Hugo churns toward
the Carolina coast in September
1989. (Photo courtesy of the
National Weather Service)*

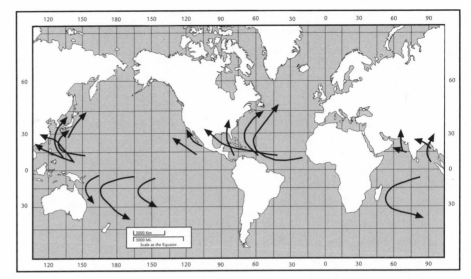

Tropical cyclone development around the world
Source: *Adapted from* Atlantic Hurricanes, *by Gordon Dunn and Banner Miller.*

There is nothing in our atmosphere that compares with their awesome fury. Arctic storms are often larger, and tornadoes may pack more violent winds, but no weather system can match the broad-scale destructive force of hurricanes. For centuries, they have left legacies of death and despair. Many tropical and temperate nations know too well the ruinous effects of these devastating storms.

In the Western Hemisphere, they are known as *hurricanes,* a term derived from the Caribbean Indian word translated as "big wind" or "storm god." *Typhoons* in the western Pacific and *cyclones* in the Indian Ocean are other names for the atmospheric phenomena we call hurricanes. All are tropical cyclones that form in the low latitudes of all tropical oceans except the South Atlantic and Southeast Pacific.

As the intense rays of the summer sun warm the ocean's surface, evaporation and conduction transfer enormous amounts of heat and moisture into the atmosphere, providing the fuel for tropical cyclones. Warm vapors rise, cool, and condense, forming billowing clouds, scattered showers, and thunderstorms. As the seedling thunderstorms multiply, they may become part of a passing *tropical wave,* a low-pressure trough that drifts westward through equatorial waters. The wave may develop into a *depression,* as thunderclouds build and barometric pressures drop. Under the right conditions, the depression may intensify into a tropical storm with gale-force winds and eventually become a full-grown hurricane.

Often, tropical depressions strengthen as they begin to show signs of rotation. The earth's spin produces the *Coriolis effect,* which causes winds within

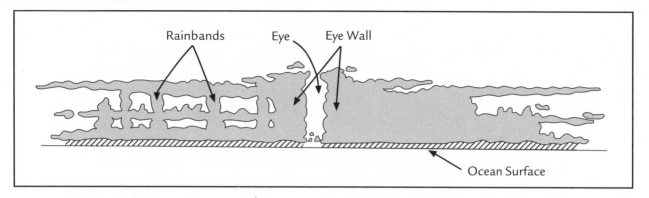

Rainbands   Eye   Eye Wall

Ocean Surface

Cross-section of a severe hurricane

A condemned cottage at Nags Head finally gives in to the sea after a strong northeaster in April 1988. (Photo by Drew Wilson; courtesy of the Outer Banks History Center)

the depression to curve and bend around the central low pressure. These curving winds help intensify the storm, as warm, moist air recharges the thunderstorms. In the Northern Hemisphere, cyclones spin counterclockwise, whereas those originating below the equator spin clockwise. Once the rotation is well defined, the storm becomes organized and takes on the character of a potential hurricane. Winds near the center of the storm increase, and a relatively calm eye develops, surrounded by ominous spiral rainbands that extend outward for many miles. When sustained winds reach 74 mph or greater, the tropical storm becomes a hurricane.

A well-developed hurricane covers thousands of square miles as it drifts across the ocean's surface. Rivers of air in the atmosphere push and steer tropical storms and hurricanes. Low-level trade winds and high-altitude steering currents join to guide these storms on what are often erratic courses. Many hurricanes appear to wobble, like a child's top spun precariously across a table. As long as they remain over warm water, tropical cyclones can strengthen and grow. To intensify, they need a good supply of fuel—the heat and moisture available to the atmosphere at sea. As they move over relatively cooler water, or over land, they lose their source of energy and begin to weaken. Often, however, hurricanes striking the coast may curve back out to sea, where they can regain their intensity and come ashore in other regions.

The heat required to fuel these storms is at its peak during the long, hot days of late summer. August and September are prime months for tropical storms in the North Atlantic, but the official hurricane season lasts from June 1 to November 30. The earliest known start for North Carolina's hurricane season was on June 3, 1825, when a major storm struck the state. One hundred years later, the latest North Carolina hurricane on record crossed Carteret County on December 2, 1925. Perhaps the most notorious of all Carolina storms, hurricane Hazel, struck in October 1954. Historically, however, most hurricanes have made landfall during the season's peak in late summer.

In an average year, we can expect more than one hundred tropical disturbances to form in the Atlantic, Gulf of Mexico, and Caribbean. Of these, only ten will reach tropical-storm intensity, and only six of these storms will become hurricanes. On average, two of these hurricanes will strike the U.S. coastline, anywhere between Texas and Maine. Some portion of North Carolina can expect to be affected by a hurricane about once every four years, based on the number of storms that have struck the state over the last century.

True hurricanes usually have tropical origins and fall within the June to November season. But other dreadful storms can strike during the winter months, featuring many of the same destructive characteristics as their tropical counterparts. These winter storms, or *northeasters*, often batter the Carolina coast with strong northeast winds that cause high tides, widespread flooding, and extensive beach erosion.

Northeasters are actually extratropical cyclones, similar in many respects to hurricanes but lacking a central warm air mass and a well-defined eye. They usually develop when low-pressure systems move out of the Gulf of Mexico and into the Atlantic, where they gain strength from the warm waters of the Gulf Stream. These winter storms are frequent visitors to the Outer Banks, sometimes stalling offshore and pounding the coast for days. The Ash Wednesday Storm of 1962 and the March Superstorm of 1993 are two classic northeasters whose destructive legacies compare with those of some of our worst hurricanes.

HURRICANE EFFECTS

Violent hurricanes and north-easters can bring awesome destruction to coastal areas, as evidenced in this scene from the Ash Wednesday Storm. (Photo courtesy of Roy Hardee)

Television coverage of modern hurricanes like Hugo and Andrew has provided graphic evidence of the violence unleashed by these storms. When powerful hurricanes strike populated areas the effects can be devastating. Their high winds leave homes and businesses with the bombed-out appearance of a war zone. The surging ocean and unyielding rain inundate coastal communities and inland rivers, flooding out homes, highways, and farmlands. The combined natural forces of wind and water sometimes take the lives of the unprepared and cause property losses in the billions of dollars.

But how does the hurricane machine deal out such destruction? Each storm may affect a region differently, but every hurricane is capable of striking in many ways. Forecasters look carefully at the measurable components of each storm to create an accurate picture of its potential for disaster.

WINDS

By definition, a tropical storm becomes a hurricane when its constant wind speeds are determined to be 74 mph or greater. At this minimal intensity, the hurricane may bring modest damage to trees, signs, roofs, and other structures. Wind gusts may exceed this level and create greater destruction in isolated areas near the center of the storm. More intense hurricanes pack much higher winds. Storms with sustained winds greater than 120 mph can cause more significant structural damage, as this is the threshold the North Carolina coastal building code sets as the design wind speed, the force newly constructed buildings must be able to withstand. As wind speeds increase, the forces they exert on a structure begin to multiply. The 120-mph winds of a major hurricane would exert about four times the force of a 60-mph wind.

Rarely, "super hurricanes" may develop with constant wind speeds of over 155 mph and gusts exceeding 200 mph. These tornado-speed velocities produce deadly consequences, as even substantial structures may be blown to pieces. Hurricane Camille, which struck near Biloxi, Mississippi, in August 1969, was just such a storm. It is estimated that Camille's winds were over 175 mph, although meteorologists concede that such extreme winds are difficult to verify. In some areas, gusts may have topped 200 mph.

In North Carolina, no super hurricanes have been verified, although extreme winds have been recorded in several storms. On August 18, 1879, winds at Cape Lookout were estimated at 168 mph, after the lighthouse keeper's *anemometer* (wind-measuring instrument) was blown away. Several estimates of 150-mph winds were reported during hurricane Hazel in 1954, and gusts of more then 100 mph were observed as Hazel tracked northward through Raleigh.

The widespread damages that result from these high winds are obvious in the aftermath of a severe hurricane. Shattered, uprooted, and fallen trees are

commonplace, affecting tall pines as well as mature hardwoods. As hurricane Hugo blazed across western North Carolina, its freakish winds damaged more than 2.7 million acres of forests in twenty-six counties, creating losses of more than $250 million in timber alone. And when trees fall, they often fall on power lines, homes, automobiles, and, sometimes, people. But the destruction from Hugo in North Carolina was only a fraction of the damage left in South Carolina, where this hurricane made landfall.

Much like trees, utility poles sometimes sway or snap in a hurricane's vio-

On the morning after hurricane Donna's visit in September 1960, merchants along Front Street in Beaufort survey their losses. The combination of high tides and destructive winds affected almost every business along the waterfront. (Photo courtesy of Roy Hardee)

Hurricane Emily's winds easily snapped these pine trees near Cape Hatteras in 1993. (Photo courtesy of Drew Wilson/ Virginian-Pilot/Carolina Coast)

Miles from the coast, this automobile dealership in Clinton lost its sign to hurricane Hazel's winds when the storm swept inland.

Hurricane Donna's winds cracked numerous utility poles in the east, including this one near Morehead City.

lent gusts. As the poles go down, they bring with them a tangled web of hot electric cables, cutting power to whole communities and threatening unsuspecting storm victims with the risk of electrocution. Utility companies are always challenged by major hurricanes, as line crews work around the clock to restore power to thousands of customers after a storm has passed.

Hurricane-force winds affect structures to varying degrees, depending upon the velocity of the wind, the exposure of the building, and the materials and methods used in the construction process. Windows can be protected by shutters or plywood (tape does nothing to stop breakage). Roof failures can occur during severe hurricanes, although proper construction techniques can limit roof damage in moderate storms. But even when all building codes are followed, there is no such thing as a "hurricane-proof" house.

Winds from Hazel were officially estimated near 150 mph in Brunswick County and continued at hurricane force as the storm sped across the state. Wind damage was heavy in thirty North Carolina counties. (Photo courtesy of News and Observer Publishing Co./ N.C. Division of Archives and History)

Unsecured lumber, tools, lawn furnishings, and other loose objects can become deadly projectiles during hurricanes.

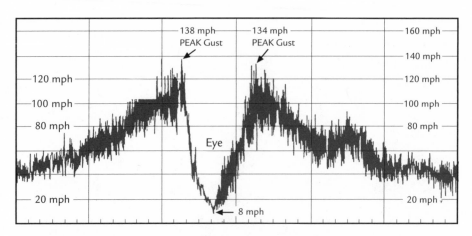

Representative anemometer record during the passing of a severe hurricane

Fierce hurricane winds have been known to topple large airplanes, derail massive freight trains, and flip mobile homes like matchboxes. Lawn furniture, lumber, and other household items become deadly projectiles when they are launched by gusts of 100-plus mph. Those who venture out into the fury of these destructive forces place their lives in jeopardy. Cleanup efforts often take weeks or months because a storm's churning winds may leave tons of debris scattered over many miles.

STORM SURGE

Although hurricanes are often feared for their tempestuous winds, their most deadly impact comes from the accompanying onslaught of water and waves. The ocean's rapid rise peaks near the time the hurricane makes landfall, creating a *storm surge* that can be devastating. The surge is usually greatest on the beaches, but the massive rush of water that overwashes the coast can flood inland sounds and rivers far beyond their banks. And, as expected, the more intense the storm, the greater the storm surge.

Our first sign of the storm surge's approach may arrive a day or more before the hurricane, as the bulging ocean begins to pile up several feet of water against hundreds of miles of coastline. Huge swells travel great distances in front of the storm, crashing on the beach and creating a roar that can be heard for miles inland. Although the skies may be clear and sunny, the ominous spectacle of evenly spaced, ten-foot swells spanning the horizon gives warning of the hurricane's approach.

Unlike the single, giant tidal waves that are miscast as hurricane threats in Hollywood films, the storm surge phenomenon may inundate the coast over a period of minutes or hours. As the hurricane churns across the open sea,

Waves literally broke through the streets of Wrightsville Beach prior to the twelve-foot storm surge that struck the island during hurricane Hazel in 1954. (Photo courtesy of the Cape Fear Museum)

the combined effects of the storm's lowered barometric pressure and strong, inward-spiraling winds create a deep, swirling column of water beneath the ocean's surface. This effect causes the sea level to rise in the vicinity of the storm, creating a dome of water that may be a few feet high in the center and one hundred miles wide. This dome of water and underlying circulation advance with the hurricane and create a dangerous surge as the storm moves over shallow water near the coast.

As the hurricane thrusts toward land, the gradually shallowing seafloor forces the water dome to rise dramatically. Powerful hurricanes produce surges that can exceed heights of twenty feet above sea level, bringing total devastation to beachfront structures. Typically, pounding waves driven by high winds ride atop the measured surge. Under these extreme conditions, it is not difficult to understand why nine out of ten hurricane-related deaths are attributed to drowning.

Although some hurricanes produce monstrous storm surges, others do not. In each storm, a variety of factors contribute to the severity of the resulting flood. The hurricane's intensity and forward speed, as well as the coincidental timing of normal astronomical high tide, determine the measured effect of the tidal surge. Geographical factors such as the curvature of the coastline and the topography of the seafloor can alter the surge's impact, by either dispersing the water dome or concentrating its destructive energy.

Historically, storm tides around the world have produced epic tragedies. In parts of Asia, the death tolls from cyclones have reached biblical proportions.

Many areas of the North Carolina coast can be affected by floods, especially portions of the Outer Banks. Streets in Kitty Hawk flooded during the Halloween storm of 1991. (Photo by Drew Wilson; courtesy of the Outer Banks History Center)

Wind-driven waves sometimes overwash the primary dunes that line the shore on North Carolina's barrier islands. After this dune was eroded in the Ash Wednesday Storm, these cottages were un-protected from the advancing tide. (Photo by Aycock Brown; courtesy of the Outer Banks History Center)

As late as 1970, a disastrous storm tide claimed several hundred thousand lives in the low coastal regions of what is now Bangladesh. Eleven thousand more perished in a cyclone that struck that region in 1984. Our hemisphere has not experienced loss of life on that scale, although great tragedies have occurred. In August 1893, a powerful hurricane surprised residents of Charleston, South Carolina, and between one and two thousand persons drowned in the rapidly rising storm tide. In October of the same year, two thousand more were lost in Louisiana as another hurricane surged across the Mississippi Delta. The great Galveston hurricane of 1900 claimed six thousand lives, most

of which were lost to the spectacular rise in sea level that occurred as the storm made landfall.

Through the years, numerous hurricanes have struck the low-lying beaches of North Carolina, some completely overwashing the barrier islands that line the coast. Often, the storm tides and hurricane winds push around the waters of the Pamlico and Albemarle Sounds, swelling rivers and tidal creeks and flooding streets and homes far from the Atlantic Ocean. High winds drive surges of water across the shallow sounds, only to rebound back to sea as the winds shift, overwashing the Outer Banks and cutting new inlets across the narrow strips of sand.

Although hurricane Hazel did not sweep over the Outer Banks, its storm surge on the Brunswick County beaches was the greatest in North Carolina's recorded history. Unfortunately, Hazel's landfall coincided with normal high tide, adding to the rise in sea level at Sunset Beach, Ocean Isle, Holden Beach, and Long Beach. Across this span of some forty miles, the storm surge ranged between sixteen and eighteen feet above mean sea level. This massive flood damaged or destroyed virtually every structure along the strand and was the focal point of one of our state's greatest natural disasters.

RAINFALL

The turbulent rush of the storm tide is not the only source of flooding associated with hurricanes. Torrential rains fall as spiral bands of storm clouds empty out across the land. These rains may pour for hours or days, depending on the forward speed of the hurricane. On average, six to twelve inches of rain

In this dramatic before-and-after sequence, the effects of hurricane Hazel's seventeen-foot storm surge on Long Beach can be seen. More than 350 cottages lined both sides of the beach road prior to October 1954 (top); after Hazel only five remained intact. Most washed into the marsh (bottom) or completely disappeared. Miles of protective dunes were flattened by the record tide. The arrow marks where the curve in the road used to be. (Photos courtesy of the U.S. Army Corps of Engineers)

Through the years many residents on the Outer Banks have adapted to the threat of rising flood-waters. Some have even prepared their homes by drilling holes through floorboards to allow the tide to enter, thus preventing the houses from floating away. (Photo courtesy of the Coastland Times*)*

can be expected as a hurricane passes nearby. Slow-moving cyclones can dump enormous amounts of rain, as Diana did in 1984, when almost fourteen inches of rain fell in Wilmington over a two-day period.

As large hurricanes track inland, flash floods can be deadly, especially in mountainous areas. Some of the most destructive floods in U.S. history were caused by the remnants of hurricane Agnes in 1972. After coming ashore on the Gulf coast of Florida, Agnes spun across Georgia and the Carolinas, crossed over the Chesapeake Bay, and bounced back through the state of New York. Heavy rains brought extensive flooding to the eastern seaboard, as numerous rivers crested at record levels. In North Carolina, Mount Mitchell recorded eleven inches of rain, and several rivers spilled over their banks. The Yadkin River crested 14.6 feet above flood level, inundating 86,000 acres of farms and homes. Across the eastern states, 122 deaths and over $2 billion in damages were attributed to the inland floods from hurricane Agnes.

TORNADOES

As if bruising winds and life-threatening floods weren't enough, hurricanes sometimes breed tornadoes that can rip through populated areas without warning. Just as large thunderheads moving across the great plains bring twisters to the Midwest, the hurricanes' spiral rainbands sometimes spawn tornadoes. Some, known as *waterspouts*, form over water, and others touch

Hurricane Ione, the third of the 1955 season to strike North Carolina, delivered record rainfall to much of the eastern part of the state. In New Bern, where forty city blocks were flooded, children explored the streets by boat after the storm. (Photo courtesy of New Bern–Craven County Public Library)

down on land, leaving behind narrow paths of concentrated destruction. Tornado winds can easily top 200 mph, and very little can withstand their menacing force. In 1967, hurricane Beulah struck the Texas coast and established a record for tornado activity. Over 150 separate twisters were reported as the hurricane made landfall and moved inland.

Tornadoes and waterspouts sometimes develop during hurricanes. (Photo courtesy of NOAA)

STORM INTENSITY

The awesome natural forces displayed by hurricanes can sometimes leave behind an equally awesome calamity: the ruinous scene of devastated homes, businesses, farmlands, and forests. But more often than not, hurricanes strike with lesser winds and moderate tides. Not all hurricanes are created equal, and their fickle nature often brings about changes in intensity with each news update. These changes can be critically important to coastal residents and forecasters who must make judgments about warnings and evacuations. All hurricanes are dangerous, but certainly some bring a greater potential for disaster than others.

In the last few decades, meteorologists have used the Saffir-Simpson scale to rate hurricane intensity. On this relative scale of one to five, a minimal hurricane with wind speeds of 74–95 mph is considered a category-one storm. At the other extreme, category-five hurricanes are worst-case events, where wind speeds top 155 mph and storm surges can exceed eighteen feet.

Category-five hurricanes are extremely rare, and only two are known to have made landfall in the United States in this century. The Labor Day Storm of 1935 washed over the Florida Keys on September 3, claiming 408 lives and punishing those remote islands with winds estimated at 200 mph. Hurricane Camille rolled into Biloxi, Mississippi, in August 1969, and then its remnants washed through Tennessee, Kentucky, and Virginia. This category-five superstorm delivered a surge of twenty-five feet at Pass Christian, Mississippi, winds estimated at over 175 mph, and a death toll that exceeded 250. Camille's rain clouds emptied out across Virginia, in some areas dumping twenty-seven

North Carolina's fishing piers are extremely vulnerable to hurricanes, as even modest storms can bring damages. (Photo by Drew Wilson; courtesy of the Outer Banks History Center)

Hurricane intensity is measured on the Saffir-Simpson scale, which categorizes a storm's severity and potential for destruction on a scale of one to five. A category-one hurricane may bring modest damage and a category-five storm is a catastrophic event. Hurricane Emily was a minimal category three when it brushed the Outer Banks and battered Cape Hatteras in 1993. (Photo courtesy of Drew Wilson/Virginian-Pilot/ Carolina Coast)

inches of rain in eight hours. Flash foods raced across the state, claiming 109 lives. In all, Camille was one of the most powerful and destructive hurricanes to strike the United States in the twentieth century.

In the United States, the tragedies brought about by Camille had been unmatched by modern storms until hurricane Andrew ravished South Florida in 1992. Andrew was a strong category four as it raced into southern Dade County, bearing down on the National Hurricane Center and the area surrounding Homestead Air Force Base. Winds gusted near 175 mph and entire communities were demolished. Andrew wiped out over 70,000 acres of mangrove forests, sank or destroyed over 15,000 boats, and left more than 250,000 homeless. Homestead was particularly hard hit, as tornado-like winds ripped apart houses and shattered mobile homes. After crossing the Florida Peninsula, Andrew returned to the waters of the Gulf of Mexico and regained much of its strength. Two days later, this killer storm was back, threatening the Louisiana coast with its second wind. In all, Andrew killed forty-three in Florida, claimed fifteen more lives in Louisiana, and cost this nation more than $25 billion—by far the most costly hurricane in American history.

Meteorologists use barometric pressure as a primary scale for determining the intensity of hurricanes—the lower the pressure, the more intense the storm. During the Labor Day Storm of 1935, a pressure reading of 26.35 inches was made on Long Key, Florida, which stood for fifty-three years as the lowest on record in the Western Hemisphere. In 1988 hurricane Gilbert, also a category five, struck Cozumel, Mexico, with devastating force. Prior to the hurricane's landfall, reconnaissance aircraft recorded a barometric pressure of

The destructive forces of hurricane Hazel's storm surge and high winds are evident in this image of the Breakers Hotel at Wilmington Beach. Hazel ranks as a category four on the Saffir-Simpson scale. (Photo courtesy of the N.C. Division of Archives and History)

26.13 inches, establishing a new record. A comparison of the barometric pressures of the most intense hurricanes to strike the United States through 1993 is included in the appendix of this book.

Category-five storms are rare—less than 1 percent of Atlantic hurricanes reach that level of intensity. In North Carolina, no category-five hurricanes are known to have made landfall, although Hazel ranked as a category four. Category-three storms are more common, striking the state on average at least once a decade. Category-two hurricanes can still bring significant damage, and lesser storms also deserve respect. Any hurricane can be dangerous, changing intensity and direction as it races unpredictably toward the coast.

OTHER FACTORS

Rating hurricanes on the Saffir-Simpson scale is important for determining their potential for destruction. But there are other factors that can contribute to the severity of a storm's impact. The orientation, forward speed, and diam-

CATEGORY	EXAMPLE	WIND AND TIDE	EFFECTS
One	Charley (1986)	Winds 74–95 mph; surge 4–5 feet above normal	No damage to building structures; most damage to unanchored mobile homes, trees, and signs. Coastal road flooding and minor pier damage.
Two	Diana (1984)	Winds 96–110 mph; surge 6–8 feet above normal	Some damage to roofing materials, doors, and windows. Considerable damage to mobile homes, trees, signs, piers, and small boats. Some coastal evacuation routes flooded.
Three	September 1933	Winds 111–130 mph; surge 9–12 feet above normal	Structural damage to some buildings; mobile homes are destroyed. Coastal structures are damaged by floating debris. Substantial regional flooding extends along rivers and sounds.
Four	Hazel (1954)	Winds 131–155 mph; surge 13–18 feet above normal	Extensive structural damage with some complete roof failures. Major damage to lower floors of structures near the shore. All terrain lower than 10 feet above sea level may be flooded, requiring massive evacuation of residential areas as much as 6 miles inland.
Five	Camille (1969)	Winds greater than 155 mph; surge more than 18 feet above normal	Complete roof failures on many residences and industrial buildings. Some complete building failures. Major damage to all structures located less than 15 feet above sea level. Massive evacuation of all residents within 10 miles of the shoreline required.

Source: National Weather Service. (Note: Surge elevations may vary locally.)

eter of an approaching hurricane can be as significant as its intensity. The timing of lunar tides and the geographical features of the region can also alter a storm's effects.

In the Atlantic, the *right-front quadrant* of a tropical cyclone presents the greatest danger to coastal residents. The combined effects of the storm's forward speed and counterclockwise rotation produce the highest winds and greatest tidal surges in areas of the coast that are hit by this portion of the storm. Typically, hurricanes approaching North Carolina arrive from the south or southeast, riding across the warm waters of the Gulf Stream. As these storms approach, their right-front quadrant is on the northeastern side.

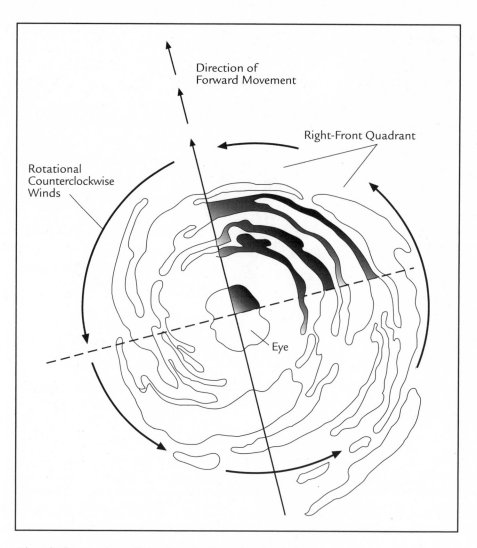

Direction of
Forward Movement

Right-Front Quadrant

Rotational
Counterclockwise
Winds

Eye

The right-front quadrant of a hurricane in the northern hemisphere

Many times, this quadrant will remain at sea as the hurricane brushes along the Outer Banks. But when a storm moves inland, the coastal region just to the right of landfall is likely to suffer the greatest damage.

The forward momentum of a hurricane as it crosses the coastline can also play a role in a storm's severity in any given area. Typically, hurricanes move across the tropical ocean at about 8–15 mph. But as they enter more temperate latitudes, they often increase forward speed, sometimes racing northward at 25–40 mph. As a storm crosses the coast, the actual measured speed of the wind could be thought of as a combination of the rotational winds of the hurricane and the contribution, either positive or negative, from the translational forward speed of the storm. Consequently, fast-moving hurricanes may bring higher winds to some locations. Slow-moving storms, on the other hand, may have lesser winds but typically dump larger amounts of rain.

Frequently, hurricanes approaching North Carolina from the south only skirt the eastern edge of the state, affecting the Outer Banks but sparing the mainland. These storms may actually make landfall near Ocracoke or Buxton while their most destructive energies remain over the Atlantic. In 1985, hurricane Gloria was just such a storm, striking Cape Hatteras and then skipping out to sea. Gloria's powerful right-front quadrant remained over the ocean while it passed, lessening the storm's destructive effects. But Gloria still ravaged the Outer Banks, causing severe beach erosion, killing one person, and causing $8 million in losses.

WATCHING THE STORMS

Amateur radio operators kept round-the-clock vigils at their stations during many of the hurricanes of the 1950s. Communications about storm movements, evacuations, and damage reports improved considerably during this period. (Photo courtesy of the Carteret County Historical Society)

Residents along the Carolina coast can expect to occasionally experience the apprehension of leaving their homes as they scramble to avoid the lashing winds and rising tides of approaching hurricanes. Costly preparations and late-night evacuations may be required of thousands of families and businesses, disrupting normal activities in numerous down-east counties. But at least today's coastal residents enjoy the benefits of forewarning. Only a few decades ago, hurricane forecasts and communications were poor, leaving some communities vulnerable. Hurricanes almost always barreled ashore without warning, often with dire consequences. Hundreds of North Carolinians have perished in rapidly rising storm tides that have left little opportunity for escape.

Before any warning systems were available, some coastal residents told the lore of a hurricane's approach. Sailors and islanders watched the skies for double moons, sundogs, and the scarlet aura of a summer sunrise. Remember the adage "Red sky at morning, sailors take warning, red sky at night, sailors delight"? Predictions of hurricanes and other catastrophes were also offered after the skies turned to night. It was once widely believed that the position and alignment of the stars and planets foretold impending hurricane tragedies.

Old-timers also monitored animal behaviors and believed some were omens of approaching storms. It's been told that shorebirds gather and livestock wander in the days preceding a hurricane. Keen observers watched the rhythm of the ocean's swells as another method of predicting incoming cyclones. But with such unreliable sources and meager communications, coastal communities stood helpless against the rapid approach of hurricanes.

During the late nineteenth century, a number of devastating hurricanes washed over the U.S. coastline, killing thousands. Frustration with these deadly storms led to the creation of the United States Weather Bureau in 1890. But it was not until the Spanish-American War of 1898 that a comprehensive hurricane-forecasting service was established. President McKinley was said to have had a greater fear of hurricanes than of attack from the Spanish navy. The warning service was extended to include shipping interests and numerous ports throughout the Caribbean, with a forecast center located in Havana, Cuba. The disastrous Galveston hurricane of 1900 shocked the nation as six thousand died, prompting the relocation of the Weather Bureau's West Indies forecast office to Washington, D.C.

But hurricane forecasting and warning was tragically ineffective in the early part of the twentieth century. During the twenties and thirties, several deadly storms struck Florida and the East Coast, killing thousands of coastal residents. Forecasts came with short notice and often never reached remote island communities. These communities were the very ones that faced the greatest risk—the horrific flood of the storm tide.

Along the boat docks of numerous coastal villages, the task of preparing for oncoming hurricanes was well practiced during the mid-1950s. Storm warnings provided adequate time for residents to "batten down the hatches." (Photo courtesy of the Carteret County Historical Society)

Along North Carolina's barrier islands, remote villages like Ocracoke and Portsmouth were especially vulnerable. Messages between these isolated areas and the mainland were transported by boat, as direct communications were not possible. One unusual method of delivering hurricane warnings was employed in the 1940s, when small planes scanned the Outer Banks and dropped warning messages in sealed containers to the isolated residents below. After receiving the news of an approaching storm, these brave families had no time to leave their island homes, only a few hours to secure their fishing boats and prepare for high winds and raging waters.

The horrible tragedies that resulted from numerous poorly forecasted hurricanes challenged scientists to better understand these phenomena. After World War II, the steering effects of the jet stream and other mechanics of cyclone development were studied intensely. At the same time, advances in technology improved the collection of weather data and led to a better understanding of hurricanes. In 1943, the first aircraft reconnaissance flight was directed into a hurricane to gather information on wind speeds, direction, and barometric pressure. Flights of the "hurricane hunters" continue today and still provide the most accurate and timely information available to forecasters.

Today, the National Hurricane Center in Coral Gables, Florida, is the nerve center for our nation's hurricane warning system. Technological advances over the last several decades have transformed hurricane forecasting and warning into an accurate, timely, lifesaving service. The advent of radar, computers, weather-watching satellites, television, and regional evacuation planning have improved the system dramatically. As a result, coastal residents can tune their televisions to the unfolding drama of an approaching hurricane often days before it strikes. It is evident that this early warning system has been effective in saving lives, as losses of life from modern hurricanes have shown an overall decline in the United States.

Refinements in the forecasting and warning system continue, with the addition of Doppler radar systems, supercomputer atmospheric modeling, and more advanced local planning for evacuation and recovery. But even today, the business of predicting when and where hurricanes will strike remains a tentative one. The unpredictable nature of these fast-moving storms can still leave coastal residents with very little time to evacuate vulnerable areas. Densely populated coastal beaches and remote islands like those of the Outer Banks can swell with traffic jams as vacationers and residents scramble to escape a rapidly moving storm. And even with today's advanced warning system, those who refuse to evacuate the barrier beaches could face the same perils endured by islanders one hundred years ago.

The National Hurricane Center in Coral Gables, Fla., watches for the development of tropical storms and hurricanes in the Atlantic, Caribbean, and Gulf of Mexico. Forecasters use satellite images and other data to project storm movements and make decisions about issuing hurricane watches and warnings. (Photo courtesy of NOAA)

Hurricane Emily will be remembered for many years on the Outer Banks. (Photo courtesy of Drew Wilson/Virginian-Pilot/Carolina Coast)

WHAT'S IN A NAME?

Popular American culture is rich with famous names. Einstein, Elvis, Oswald, and Madonna—all are household words that evoke vivid images of colorful characters. Also part of our recent past are such well-known names as Hazel, Camille, Hugo, and Andrew. For many, these names conjure up nightmarish memories of tropical terrorism. The naming of hurricanes and tropical storms began in the early 1950s, in an effort to manage storm tracking, provide historical reference, and alert and involve the general public. Often, these storms developed their own "personalities," which are forever linked to the names they received. This personification of disaster may help us better understand and cope with the emotional scars left by hurricanes.

In the eighteenth and nineteenth centuries, very few hurricanes were given names. Sometimes, extreme storms were named for the islands they devastated, the ships they sank, or the religious holidays nearest the time of their approach. The Cuba Hurricane of 1811, the Santa Ana Storm of 1825, and Racer's Storm in 1837 are some of the few early hurricanes that were given names. But most early storms are known only for the dates of their occurrences, such as the Great Storm of 1750 or the Great Wind of 1885. With so few early hurricanes identified by name, references and comparisons were somewhat difficult for those who kept historical records.

In the early days of hurricane tracking in the twentieth century, references to storms were made by their position at sea — the latitude and longitude of the latest ship report. This numerical system proved to be quite confusing, especially when several tropical disturbances were active at the same time. Eventually, military weathermen began using code names for storms in alphabetic sequence — Adam, Baker, Charlie, and so on — which made each storm easier to distinguish and track. In 1953, a system was adopted that used women's names to identify individual tropical storms and hurricanes, and that practice continued through the 1970s. In 1979, women's groups and several nations lobbied the World Meteorological Organization to change the naming system to include men's names and names of international origin. A complete list of names is now cycled with each hurricane season and then repeated every seven years. The names of significant hurricanes, like Andrew and Hugo, are retired, never to be used again. This international system of identification has proven effective in eliminating confusion and promoting awareness in coastal communities.

EARLY NORTH CAROLINA HURRICANES,
1526–1861

Records of storms and hurricanes are widely scattered throughout the history of colonial North Carolina. These early accounts are clearly incomplete, as there were certainly numerous storms that occurred during the seventeenth, eighteenth, and nineteenth centuries for which no significant record exists. Thanks to research completed by Charles Carney, Albert Hardy, and James Stevenson of the National Weather Service, early hurricane reports have been compiled for North Carolina. Portions of these records are included here as part of a sampler of our hurricane history. But be reminded that North Carolina has been struck, on average, by one hurricane every four years over the past century. We can expect that many severe hurricanes not mentioned in this chronology have assaulted the Tar Heel state.

In the age of the New World explorations and the colonization that followed, great storms often ravaged ships and settlements. The first Europeans to explore the Carolina coast may have approached during a violent hurricane. The Italian adventurer Giovanni da Verrazano sailed into North Carolina waters in 1524 and, after enduring a storm, charted the first shoal as the Cape of Feare. Two years later, in 1526, a large Spanish expedition led by Lucas de Ayllon came to the Cape of Feare in search of gold. After wrecking his ship during a "loathsome gale," de Ayllon and his men camped in the vicinity of Bald Head Island. There they built a new ship, believed to be the first ever constructed by Europeans in the New World.

After receiving a royal charter to establish a colony in the New World in 1585, Englishman Sir Walter Raleigh sent out an expedition that landed on Roanoke Island. Ralph Lane was named governor of the settlement, which consisted of a fort and several homes. The following year, Sir Francis Drake cruised into Carolina waters on his way back to England from St. Augustine. He brought his great fleet of twenty-three ships to the struggling Roanoke colony to replenish badly needed supplies and to offer Governor Lane a new ship. On June 13, 1586, a four-day hurricane scattered Drake's fleet and wrecked many of his ships. Lane later reported that "in the terrible storm he [Drake] had undergone more dangers from shipwreck in his desire to bring aid to us than all his previous engagements with the Spaniards." Lane and Drake later returned to England, bringing to an abrupt end the colony known as the Roanoke Hundred.

Still determined to establish a colony in the New World, Raleigh dispatched another group of colonists to Roanoke in 1587. This new group was led by Captain John White, whose granddaughter was Virginia Dare, the first English child born in America. This second attempt to settle on the Carolina coast was also a failure. Governor White sailed to England for desperately needed supplies and returned to the Outer Banks in 1590. Upon his arrival on Roanoke Island, the colonists could not be found and their homes had

(Page 33)
Ships founder in a storm off the coast of Hatteras. The area, notorious for its dangerous shoals, became known as the Graveyard of the Atlantic. (Engraving from the Illustrated News, *April 23, 1853; courtesy of the North Carolina Collection, University of North Carolina at Chapel Hill)*

vanished. White discovered only a wooden palisade and the word "Croatan" carved in a nearby tree. Some have speculated that the fate of the Lost Colony of Roanoke may be linked to a hurricane disaster. Contributing to the theory, in which a great storm surge swept through the settlement, four cannon, iron bars, and other metal debris were found around the site. Heavy objects may have been left behind while homes and ships were scattered by the tides. This theory is only one of many that have been offered on the mystery of the lost colony.

Throughout the next two centuries, coastal settlements slowly developed in the East, and with the exception of Native American peoples, the region was very sparsely populated. Few records or reports exist of the many hurricanes that must have affected the early colonial settlements. Through the seventeenth century, only three hurricanes are known to have affected North Carolina, although many others must have struck the region. On September 6, 1667, a severe storm dragged through southern Virginia destroying crops and buildings. It is assumed that this hurricane passed over the Outer Banks prior to its move up the Chesapeake. Rains from this storm were said to have lasted for twelve days.

The Great Storm of August 18, 1750, was responsible for numerous reports of damage along the Carolina coast. New inlets were cut through barrier islands, and five ships of the Spanish Flota, a fleet sent to plunder coastal settlements, were reported washed ashore or wrecked. Then, in 1752, another fateful storm tracked from Charleston, South Carolina, up the coastline and also destroyed many ships. But this hurricane's most infamous result was the flood and destruction of the Onslow County seat. The town of Johnston, named after Governor Gabriel Johnston, was built on a bluff in an area now known as Old Town Point, part of present-day Camp Lejeune. During this late September storm, the Onslow County Courthouse was completely destroyed, and all of the county's records and deeds were lost. Portions of the courthouse were said to have washed "across the New River, there two miles wide." Virtually every building in town was reportedly wrecked, and eight residents were killed. So great was the loss at Johnston that the town was abandoned and a new county seat was established at Wantland's Ferry (known today as Jacksonville). The only structure that remained at Johnston was the jail, as reported in court documents in 1753: "Whereas the prison is not sufficient since the storm and as no one lives near it, it is the opinion of the court that the sheriff may make a prison of his own house or plantation till further provision is made."

According to legend, rising water from the hurricane of 1752 swept a small boy, about four years old, across the river, where he was saved from the deadly tide. Barely able to speak after his frightening ordeal, the only word he could say was "Hadnot." The point of land where he was found was then named Hadnot Point, which is also part of present-day Camp Lejeune. The boy's name was Charles Hadnot, and he was adopted by the county.

A severe hurricane in September 1761 washed over the southern coast of North Carolina. Once again many ships were wrecked and homes were destroyed. A new inlet was cut near Bald Head Island at a location known as "Haul-over." Nearly one mile wide and eighteen feet deep, this inlet remained open for more than a hundred years.

Lengthy reports were made of a devastating hurricane that struck North Carolina on September 6, 1769. The effects of this storm were most severe in the region from Smithville (known today as Southport) through New Bern, the colonial state capital. The Brunswick County Courthouse was reportedly blown down, along with thousands of trees. In New Bern, the tide was said to have risen twelve feet higher than "ever before." Many homes and stores were destroyed, and one entire street of houses was washed away, along with several residents. In a letter to the Earl of Hillsborough, Governor Tryon wrote: "New Bern is really now a spectacle, her streets full of the tops of houses, timber, shingles, dry goods, barrels and hogsheads, empty most of them, rubbish, . . . in so much that you can hardly pass along; a few days ago so flourishing and thriving — it shows the instability of all sublunary things. . . . In short, my Lord, the inhabitants never knew so violent a storm; every herbage in the gardens had their leaves cut off. This hurricane is attributed to the effect of a blazing planet or star that was seen both from New Bern and here, rising in the east for several nights between the 26th and 31st of August, its stream was very long and stretched upwards towards the west."

Notable hurricanes struck the New Bern area again in 1803, 1815, 1821, and 1825. On September 3 and 4, 1815, a powerful hurricane surprised coastal residents and made landfall near Swansboro. According to a report in the *Raleigh Minerva*, the storm caused great damage and loss of life in Onslow. Mr. Nelson's home on Brown's Banks was swept away during the storm surge, taking with it four of his children. The father and one son survived by clinging to the wreck of their house as it carried them nearly twelve miles to Stone's Bay on the New River.

A rare early June hurricane swept through North Carolina in 1825, leaving destruction in its wake from Cuba to New England. Tides at Adam's Creek rose fourteen feet, and surging water flooded downtown New Bern. More than twenty ships were driven ashore on Ocracoke Island, twenty-seven near Washington, and dozens more from Wilmington to Cape Lookout.

On August 24 and 25, 1827, another powerful hurricane moved across the state, with reported effects from Cape Hatteras to Winston-Salem. During the peak of this storm, the Diamond Shoals Lightship broke away from its anchors and drifted southward to Portsmouth. Two of the lightship's crew were washed overboard and lost at sea. After this storm, the treacherous Diamond Shoals were without a signal light for several years.

The year 1837 was significant in North Carolina's hurricane history, as three storms are known to have struck the state between August and November. The hurricane that inundated the coastal region on August 19 of that year most likely came ashore near Wilmington. This storm brought tremendous rains to the region, and rivers crested at record levels. It was reported that there was not a bridge left standing between Wilmington and Waynesboro (known today as Goldsboro). According to one eyewitness report from the storm, "The gale was certainly the most violent we have witnessed and the quantity of water . . . greater than has ever been known."

In October of the same year, a long-lived hurricane dubbed Racer's Storm wandered from the Yucatan Peninsula to the Texas coast, across the Gulf states and Florida and into the Atlantic. On October 9, 1837, this storm crossed over the Outer Banks, sinking numerous ships. One of this hurricane's worst tragedies occurred with the loss of the steamship *Home*, as 90 of the ship's 130 passengers were lost at sea. Three weeks after Racer's Storm had passed, the third hurricane of the season bruised the Outer Banks.

In 1842, two hurricanes punished coastal North Carolina. Damage was recorded from Wilmington to Currituck after the first, a July storm that sunk numerous ships along the coastline. The most severe damage was reported from Portsmouth northward along the Outer Banks, where livestock drowned and homes were washed away. For residents of these remote islands, this hurricane is believed to have been one of the most severe on record. Less than thirty days later, another hurricane swept over the Outer Banks, again bringing destruction to the region. Among the losses were three ships: the *Congress*, which wrecked at Cape Hatteras, the *Pioneer* at Ocracoke, and the *Kilgore* at Currituck.

The hurricane that approached the North Carolina coast on September 6, 1846, was both intense and slow moving. A remarkable surge of water, driven by continuous northeast winds, pushed far into the Pamlico and Albemarle Sounds, flooding rivers and creeks for miles inland. Then, as the hurricane passed and its winds rotated to the southwest, this massive expanse of water rushed back toward the sea, overwashing the Outer Banks from west to east. On the night of September 7, a new inlet was created by these events, known today as Hatteras Inlet. The next day, a second inlet was formed just south of Roanoke Island. This inlet soon became navigable and was named Oregon Inlet for the first large boat to pass through it, the *Oregon*. For years after this storm, sounds and bays that had always been freshwater were said to contain oysters, stingrays, and other saltwater creatures. In addition to wrecking homes and ships, this amazing hurricane literally reshaped the geography of the Outer Banks.

The "perfect tempest" that struck the Cape Fear region on a full moon in September 1856 also delivered a massive storm surge. Heavy crop damage was reported, as fields were flooded with salt water from the hurricane's incredible tide. Prior to this storm, Wrightsville Beach was said to have been covered with groves of live oaks. As this hurricane made landfall, the surging ocean overwashed Wrightsville. The waves uprooted and swept away most of the oaks and left only a few trees standing. Of those that remained, most died within a few days due to the invasion of salt water. Reports of waves breaking one-half mile inland from the sound at an elevation of thirty feet have led to speculation that this hurricane's floods may have been some of the worst in North Carolina's history.

Just after the battle of Fort Sumter in April 1861, President Lincoln declared a commercial and military blockade of all southern ports, and the Civil War began. Within months, the Union navy positioned a fleet of seventy-five vessels along the Carolina coast, which was at that time the largest ever assembled by a U.S. commander. On November 1, a terrific late-season hurricane scattered the fleet and brought a major setback to the Union command. At least two vessels sank, and several sailors drowned. Some of the ships were wrecked on North Carolina beaches, where Confederates were able to salvage their goods.

TAR HEEL TRAGEDIES,
1875–1900

Weather station at Cape Hatteras, ca. 1890. (Photo courtesy of the Outer Banks History Center)

Coastal North Carolina enjoyed a prosperous period through the late nineteenth century, as many cities and towns became linked by waterway, railroad, and telegraph. Growing agricultural and fishing industries provided work for residents, and the lure of the ocean attracted an increasing number of Piedmont vacationers. The coastal population was growing at a steady pace, even though great storms frequently battered eastern communities.

The twenty-five-year period that ended the century was a particularly active one for hurricanes in North Carolina. At least eleven struck the state during that time, and five of those were severe. On several occasions, two or more struck the coast during the same year, sometimes only weeks apart. This kind of double whammy occurred in 1882, 1893, and again in 1899.

The recording and reporting of information about hurricanes improved significantly during this period. Weather stations positioned across the state made records of winds and events, building an overall picture of each storm's movement and character. Improvements in communications brought more accurate and timely reports of hurricane damages to newspapers in the East. As a result, we know many more details about the hurricanes of the late nineteenth century than those of earlier times.

SEPTEMBER 17, 1876

Early on the morning of September 17, 1876, a powerful hurricane inundated the Cape Fear region, bringing significant damage to Smithville, Brunswick,

A historical marker reminds visitors of the movements of the Providence Methodist Church in Swan Quarter.

and Wilmington. High winds disabled the recently installed anemometers at Wilmington and Cape Hatteras, leaving no good record of the storm's top winds. In Wilmington, this hurricane was called "the worst in many years," and water rose "unprecedentedly" high in the sounds. Many large trees were downed, bridges were washed away, and two railroad box cars were said to have been driven uphill by the wind. Waterfowl were forced inland, and marsh hens were said to have been killed with sticks as they sought refuge in homes and barns. By nine o'clock that morning, the skies over Smithville (Southport) were "as dark as any night" as the storm's heavy rain clouds spun their way northward.

The impact of the 1876 storm was felt far beyond the Cape Fear region. In Onslow County, a military camp established to install and maintain the area's first telegraph line was destroyed by the rising tide, and two soldiers drowned. From Ocracoke to Rocky Mount, reports were gathered of killed and injured citizens. Although this storm brought many tragedies to the state, it also is credited with bringing a minor miracle to Hyde County.

It seems that in the town of Swan Quarter, in the spring of 1876, the local Methodists had decided to build a new church. After selecting a desirable location near the center of town, the congregation was displeased to learn that the land's owner, Sam Sadler, had no interest in giving up his property. Even after the offer was increased, Sadler refused to sell. Determined to construct a new church, the citizens obtained another piece of property on the edge of town, where they built a small frame building. The congregation was satisfied, and their new church was dedicated on September 14 — the same day a major hurricane was churning past Cuba on its way toward the Carolina coast.

As the hurricane spun across the state, winds drove high waters across Pamlico Sound and piled them on the shores of Hyde County. Swan Quarter was flooded with five feet of water. Homes and businesses were deluged and wrecked, and the town's fishing fleet was severely damaged. But even with all the destruction around them, the residents of Swan Quarter were most alarmed by an apparent act of divine intervention.

During the storm, rising tides in the street had lifted the small frame church off its foundation and floated it toward the center of town. After the waters receded, residents were astonished to see that the new church had settled down on Sam Sadler's land, just as they had originally planned. Sadler was also impressed: he later signed a deed and gave his land to the Methodist church. Today, a sign stands in front of the Providence Church, reminding visitors that this was the church "Moved by the Hand of God."

AUGUST 18, 1879

In the late nineteenth century, seaside resorts in coastal North Carolina were frequented by vacationers from across the state, just as they are today. One of the more popular resort destinations was the prestigious Atlantic Hotel in Beaufort. Built in 1859 by Captain Josiah Pender, the hotel was constructed on pilings over the water at the foot of Pollock Street. During the Civil War the resort was transformed into a hospital, but by 1870 the Atlantic Hotel was again hosting vacationers. The three-story structure featured broad verandas on each level and numerous windows to catch the prevailing summer breeze off the water. Its charm and location attracted business leaders and families who traveled by train from as far west as Asheville. The hotel did not endure for long, however, as it became the scene of a tragic episode of North Carolina's hurricane history.

On August 17, 1879, preparations were under way for the arrival of a special convention in Beaufort. The *Raleigh Observer* on August 16 announced: "Major Perry of the Atlantic Hotel, Beaufort, will give a Grand Dress Ball in honor of the North Carolina Press Association on Thursday night, August 21. . . . Major Perry will spare no pains in making it one of the handsomest of the season." The hotel was already brimming with guests, including Governor Thomas J. Jarvis, his wife, and numerous prominent friends from around the state. The Gatlings of Raleigh, the Stronachs of Wilson, and the Hughes of New Bern joined the governor and his family. On the evening of Sunday the seventeenth, the hotel guests retired with no knowledge of the powerful hurricane that was soon to strike.

By 1:00 A.M. on August 18, heavy rains and gusting winds were sweeping over the North Carolina coastline. By 3:00 A.M., many Beaufort residents were pacing in their homes as the winds increased dramatically and the storm's surge began flooding Front Street. The hurricane was intense at Cape Lookout, where a Signal Corps officer reported:

> The howling of the wind and the rushing of the water past the station woke us at 5 A.M., 18th. Velocity at this time being 80 mph. and rapidly increasing. The rain pouring down in torrents, the sea rushing past the house at a fearful rate and rising rapidly. It soon undermined the Signal Service Stable, The Light House Establishment Store House and a cookhouse, which were blown down and carried away by the rushing tide. The Signal Service mule which became loose when the stable washed away tried to come to the dwelling house but could not face the raging storm; she turned and rushed into the foaming billows. The fence around the lighthouse next went carrying the keeper's fuel along with it. The whaling schooner *Seychell* of Provincetown, Mass., 50 tons, Capt. Cook, fishing in these waters, was at anchor in the Hook, parted her chains. . . . At the time the vessel crossed Wreck Point she was drawing 12 feet of water, thus showing the tide to have been fuller than ever known at this place.

Amazingly, the signal officers at Cape Lookout were able to survive the storm and were witness to the highest winds ever reported in North Carolina. The station's anemometer cups were blown away at 6:35 A.M., at which time the register showed a velocity of 138 mph. The tides continued rising and the winds steadily climbed until 7:35 A.M., when an estimate was made of 168 mph. Anemometers were also reported destroyed at Fort Macon, Portsmouth, Hatteras, Kitty Hawk, and Cape Henry, Virginia.

In Beaufort, the guests at the Atlantic Hotel were stirred by the storm in the early morning hours. One visitor reported: "About 4 o'clock A.M. the tide had risen very much, and the wind was so strong that it was impossible to stand. But those who had witnessed repeated storms at Beaufort told us there was nothing to fear. At about 5 o'clock, the water had risen to the floor of the hotel, and it was thought best to remove the children and ladies. This determination was taken so late that many of them had hardly time to dress, and a few were not dressed."

Many of the hotel guests escaped with a few clothes or belongings and were forced to swim or wade through the chest-deep waters that had engulfed Front Street. The surging tide washed boats and debris as far into town as Broad Street. Most of the hotel refugees were taken in by the good people of Beaufort, where they were sheltered in hallways and kitchens.

As the hurricane's surge continued to rise, the Atlantic Hotel and other waterfront dwellings began to crumble. In the chaos that followed, the Beaufort waterfront was the scene of heroic rescues and great tragedies. The entire

Stronach family was saved from the collapsing hotel by a black man, Palmer Davis. Davis carried the Stronach children in his arms through chest-deep water and falling debris. He also rescued the teenaged daughter of Seaton Gales of Raleigh. Davis was later recognized by Governor Jarvis as the hero of the hour, although there were others who risked their lives in the dreadful storm.

The Hester brothers from Morehead City were also credited with saving lives as they helped several guests to safety. Henry Congleton, a local boat-hand, drowned in the tide as he attempted to rescue desperate vacationers from the top floor of the hotel. Two young men from New Bern, Owen Guion and Justice Disosway, were among those trapped on the hotel's third floor. They apparently made a last-minute escape when they jumped into the rising water, clinging to their mattresses with money in their mouths.

In addition to Congleton, two other men drowned in the collapse of the Atlantic Hotel: John Dunn of New Bern, a guest at the time, and John D. Hughes, a local young man who was one of the first to offer assistance to frightened vacationers. After rescuing several guests from the second and third floors, Hughes returned to the hotel during the peak of the storm. Thinking he saw a young woman in a window, he again approached the structure, just as battering waves and wind caused the hotel to collapse. His death was in vain, however, as he had apparently mistaken the window's shimmering curtains for the nightgown of a woman.

Among those who escaped the hotel with no time to spare were Governor Jarvis and his wife. It's been told that the governor, like many other survivors, lost all of his personal belongings and was forced to flee in his pajamas with his shoes in his hand. In the chaos of the escape, his shoes were lost, but he managed to lead his family to the safety of a cottage several blocks away.

After the storm passed and the tide receded, the Beaufort waterfront was piled high with the wreckage of the night. Trunks of damaged goods littered Front Street along with lumber and broken skiffs. Crowds of dazed people, many of them barefooted, sifted through the rubble in search of lost belongings. Thousands of dollars worth of jewels were reportedly lost in the destruction of the Atlantic Hotel. Governor Jarvis called out fifty men from the garrison at Fort Macon to guard the property strewn about the waterfront.

The citizens of Beaufort took in more than 150 refugees and offered them clothes, shoes, and whatever food was available. Governor Jarvis, in need of proper clothing, was given a sailor suit that had last been worn in the War of 1812. No shoes could be found that would fit his large feet, so he wore a pair of oversized boots. Mrs. Jarvis borrowed a calico housecoat and was thankful to be dressed for the trip back to Raleigh.

On the morning of August 19, the refugees were transported by boat to Morehead City, where they boarded a train to take them home. At New Bern, a large crowd had gathered at the station to express sympathy to Major and Mrs. Hughes for the tragic loss of their son. At 8:30 P.M. the train arrived at the station in Goldsboro, where forty editors of the North Carolina Press Association had gathered to meet the survivors. The press association had canceled their trip to the coast upon news of the hurricane and instead were meeting at Goldsboro's Gregory Hotel. The newsmen would later report on the weariness of the group and the tragedies of the storm.

Upon their arrival in Raleigh, Governor Jarvis encouraged the remaining survivors to gather at the Yarborough House Hotel for refreshments. There the storm-battered group made a toast to their survival, and the reception lasted into the night. One newsman reported that the governor looked "as weather-beaten as he used to after one of Lee's campaigns." That evening discussions about rebuilding the Atlantic Hotel began. Apparently, the idea was modified, as the New Atlantic Hotel was not built in Beaufort but in Morehead City, where it became a vacation landmark for many years.

The devastating effects of the great hurricane of 1879 were felt far beyond the Beaufort waterfront. The storm apparently made landfall near Wilmington, crossed the Pamlico Sound, and returned to the Atlantic near Norfolk, Virginia. From there it recurved to the north and brought record tides to Atlantic City and Boston. Dozens of ships were wrecked from Smithville (Southport) to Cape Cod. But by far, the storm's greatest effects were evident in eastern Carteret County.

In Morehead City, the losses were heavy and included one thousand feet of railroad track, the Morehead Market House, several windmills, a Methodist church, the city wharves, and dozens of shops and homes. Virtually every structure lost its chimney in the 150-mph gusts. Thomas Webb, a night watchman at the railway depot, nearly drowned when the rapidly rising water separated him from the mainland. He saved himself by tying his body to a drifting platform with his pants. When he was later found, exhausted, he had lost most of his clothes in the raging wind and water.

The hurricane's storm surge opened at least two inlets on Bogue Banks, just west of Fort Macon. Great destruction was reported on the barrier island communities of Diamond City and Portsmouth. Beaufort Inlet was reshaped, as almost eight hundred yards of sand were washed away on the western end of Shackleford Banks. Twenty-one dwellings were leveled in the town of Smyrna, and other communities suffered great destruction, including Cedar Island, Ocracoke, Hatteras, and Kitty Hawk.

Stories of the great hurricane of 1879 have been passed down to the families of those who survived it. Much was written about this storm's severity and destruction, and some labeled it the "worst ever." But labels can be deceiving, as each generation may endure a tragic hurricane and then describe it as incomparable. Other hurricanes that struck the North Carolina coast may have had greater winds or higher tides, but to the seaside vacationers in 1879, this storm was the worst.

SEPTEMBER 9, 1881

On September 9, 1881, a severe hurricane struck near Smithville (Southport) and curved northward through Wilmington on a path through Norfolk, Virginia. Witnesses in Smithville reported this storm to be the most violent in fifty years, as the town was "covered with fallen trees, scattered fences, and the debris of demolished buildings. All pilot boats in the harbor were sunk, and loaded vessels driven ashore."

At Wrightsville Beach, the hurricane passed around noon, its winds changing direction from the east upon approach to the west after passing. These western winds brought the greatest destruction, "blowing with redoubled fury, crushing buildings and tearing up the largest trees." At Wilmington, the anemometer was disabled after the recorder measured a four-minute constant wind of 90 mph. Property damage in the Wilmington area was estimated to be $100,000.

1882

The 1882 hurricane season was active all across North Carolina. A great hurricane came ashore on the Gulf Coast on September 9, washed through Georgia and South Carolina, and moved into the Tar Heel state near Charlotte on the eleventh. After crossing to the east, this powerful storm returned to sea near the Chesapeake Bay. Great rains fell and violent winds blew, affecting the Carolina coastline from Cape Fear to Currituck. Fences, chimneys, and large trees were toppled across the East.

Less than two weeks later, another hurricane struck the state. A cyclone crossed Cape Lookout on September 22, bringing heavy rains to the eastern counties while tracking through the Pamlico and Albemarle Sounds on its way to Virginia. Swollen rivers washed out several bridges, including a trestle on the Wilmington and Weldon Railway. One train reportedly crashed in the washout, seriously injuring the crew aboard. Crop damage from the battering rains was heavy. Tarboro reported the heaviest rainfall since 1842, and some areas reported almost eight inches within a few hours.

Three weeks later, the third tropical weather event of the season brushed past the Carolina coast. On October 11, heavy rains fell throughout the day in Wilmington, as the storm apparently remained at sea. Damage from this storm was minimal along the southern coast.

SEPTEMBER 11, 1883

In September 1883, a violent hurricane made landfall near Smithville and brought punishing winds to the Cape Fear region. On the morning of the eleventh, maximum winds in Southport were recorded at 93 mph, with gusts over 110. Newspaper reports described a constant gale of over 80 mph that lasted for more than seven hours. Even in the inland portions of Brunswick County, trees and foliage appeared frostbitten after the storm because of the salt spray carried off the ocean by the winds. Trees, fences, and telegraph lines were downed, and there was severe crop damage as far inland as Harnett County. Wind-driven water pushed far up the Cape Fear River, flooding large portions of its western banks. The Hotel Brunswick in Smithville served as a shelter for the women and children of the area.

Among the losses were several pilot boats and other craft, many of which broke their moorings and were scattered by the storm. The Frying Pan Shoals Lightship was torn from its anchors and came ashore near Myrtle Grove Sound. Countless other schooners and barks were either grounded or sunk. The thirty-three passengers aboard the steamer *City of Atlanta* survived a frightening ordeal at sea during the hurricane. Battered, but with all accounted for, the disabled steamship was towed into Smithville after the storm. Several drownings were reported from other wrecked ships, and many others died in homes that either were flooded or had collapsed during the violent gale. In all, fifty-three North Carolinians are known to have lost their lives in this hurricane, more than in any storm in the state's history.

AUGUST 25, 1885

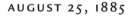

On August 24, 1885, a powerful hurricane raced through the Bahamas and made landfall near Savannah, Georgia. As it curved to the northeast, this storm washed over the South Carolina coast, claiming twenty-one lives on its way north. On September 25, the hurricane passed just west of Wilmington and continued its northeastern arc toward Cape Hatteras. At 5:15 P.M. the anemometer in Smithville was blown away after a reading of 98 mph. Within the next half hour, winds were estimated to have surpassed 125 mph at that location.

Destruction from this cyclone was reported along the southern coast and from inland counties as well. Crop destruction was heavy and many ships were grounded. Damage in Smithville was estimated to have exceeded $100,000, but the destruction in Charleston, South Carolina, approached $1.7 million. After the heavy losses on the Atlantic coast from the 1885 storm, a weather-reporting network was proposed for the West Indies and Mexico.

AUGUST 27–29, 1893

The year 1893 was deadly for hurricanes. Of the three powerful cyclones that struck the United States between August and October, two brought catastrophic destruction and great loss of life to the Carolinas.

The Great Hurricane of 1893 caused horrible flooding as it came ashore near Hilton Head, South Carolina, and totally inundated the low-lying communities of the South Carolina coast. Between one and two thousand people were believed to have drowned as this hurricane's massive storm surge surprised residents and reshaped the coastal islands. Sometimes called the Sea Islands Hurricane of 1893, this great disaster left more than thirty thousand homeless. For more than nine months, many of the storm's refugees survived on a ration of "a peck of grits and a pound of pork, per family, per week."

The Sea Islands Hurricane charted a course that would be followed by hurricane Hugo almost one century later. After killing thousands at the coast, the storm moved inland, passing through Charlotte before curving to the northeast. The massive size of this hurricane brought 72-mph winds to Wilmington, even though the more powerful winds remained near the storm's center, almost 150 miles inland. A newspaper in Kernersville reported: "A terrific cyclone struck here at five o'clock this morning. A hundred houses wrecked and a woman killed. Many were injured. Factories, stores and residences were unroofed and some were blown away."

Along the coast, the northern edges of the storm surge pushed into the Cape Fear region. At Wilmington, "the river tide was the highest ever known here. All the wharves being submerged, a number of vessels were wrecked on the coast." As the hurricane spun across the state and into Virginia, heavy rains of three to eight inches were reported at virtually all North Carolina stations.

OCTOBER 13, 1893

Six weeks after the Sea Islands Hurricane, another great hurricane entered North Carolina from the south. On October 13, this storm came ashore near Myrtle Beach and beat a path through Raleigh, a pattern similar to the track of hurricane Hazel, which would follow in 1954.

Once again, flooding on the southern coast was of record proportions. Along the Wilmington waterfront, wharves that had been submerged in the previous storm were washed away and ruined. The overflowing tide in downtown Wilmington was reported to be the greatest ever, measuring sixteen inches higher than the previous high mark established in 1853.

Crop damage from both of the 1893 hurricanes was severe. Many homes, farms, and businesses were still recovering from the August storm when the

During the late nineteenth century, many gallant rescues were performed by the crews of lifesaving stations along North Carolina's Outer Banks. (Photo courtesy of the Outer Banks History Center)

October hurricane carved a path through the state. Twenty-two North Carolinians died in the later storm, and the death toll for the two hurricanes was near forty.

AUGUST 16–18, 1899

Six years after the 1893 season, North Carolina was again ravaged by two hurricanes in the same year. And, once again, these great storms made landfall in August and October. This time, however, both hurricanes made direct hits on the North Carolina coastline: one across the Outer Banks and the other just below Wilmington.

The Great Hurricane of August 1899 is often referred to as San Ciriaco and was one of the most powerful cyclones to move through the western Atlantic in the nineteenth century. It was named by the people of Puerto Rico, where it crossed without warning on August 8, killing hundreds. The following day, the hurricane swept over the Dominican Republic and then brushed northern Cuba on the tenth. Its north-westward movement brought it near Florida's prized oceanfront resorts, and on August 13, the gently curving storm swept past the Fort Lauderdale region. As it followed the warm waters of the Gulf Stream, its continued movement might have carried it east of Cape Hatteras and out of harm's way. But on the morning of August 16, its forward speed slowed considerably, its direction changed to the northwest, and it increased in strength as it moved toward Cape Lookout.

On the morning of August 17, 1899, San Ciriaco swept over the lower banks near Diamond City. Reports of great destruction from Beaufort to Nags Head were later printed in newspapers across the country. In Carteret County, the island communities of Shackleford Banks, Diamond City, and Portsmouth were especially hard hit. These fishing villages were settled by hardy families who were accustomed to foul weather and remote lifestyles. But numerous hurricanes and northeasters near the end of the century had tested the endurance of the people known as "Ca'e Bankers." These storms left drifts of barren sand that replaced the rich soils of their gardens, and saltwater overwash killed trees and contaminated drinking wells. These communities had begun to see a decline in population prior to 1899, largely due to the unwelcome effects of hurricanes.

For the residents of Diamond City and Shackleford, the San Ciriaco hurricane was the final blow. Few if any of the homes in these island villages escaped the rushing storm tide that swept over the banks. First, the waters rose from the soundside, as northeast winds pounded the islands during the hurricane's approach. Then, as the storm passed, the winds shifted hard to the southwest, surging the ocean's tide over the dunes until the waters met. Cows, pigs, and chickens drowned, all fishing equipment was destroyed, and many homes were ruined. The aftermath was a truly ghastly scene, as battered caskets and bones lay scattered, unearthed by the hurricane's menacing storm surge.

Following the San Ciriaco storm, the people of Diamond City and Shackleford Banks gathered their remaining belongings and searched for new places to live. Many moved to the mainland, settling in Marshallberg, Broad Creek, and the Promised Land section of Morehead City. Others moved down to the island of Bogue Banks and became squatters among the dunes of Salter Path. But most chose to relocate within sight of their former community, three miles across the sound on Harker's Island. Some even salvaged their island homes, floating them across the water on barges and repositioning them on new foundations.

One of the great tragedies of the hurricane of August 1899 fell upon several families from down-east Carteret County. August was mullet fishing time, and a large group of men gathered their nets, tents, and provisions for a two-week expedition to Swan Island, just as they did each summer. Their means of transportation was a small dead-rise skiff, twenty-one feet long and about five feet wide. Each shallow skiff could carry two men and their equipment, and each craft featured a small sail on a removable mast. These shallow draft boats provided effective transport around the protected waters of Core Sound.

This particular August, the group of twenty fishermen had already established their camp on the remote island when the first signs of the San Ciriaco hurricane were recognized. At first, the brisk winds and gathering clouds appeared to be just a good "mullet blow," which would get the fish moving. But on the morning of August 17, the tide was unusually high, and heavy rains began to sweep through the sound. Alarmed by the rising water, the fishermen considered leaving but chose to stay on the island for fear of the ever-increasing winds. They were forced to pack all of their nets and supplies aboard their skiffs, as the tides washed completely over the island. They moored their skiffs as close together as they could and crouched under their canvas sails for protection from the driving rain. This proved useless, however, as they soon had to bail the water that rapidly filled their boats.

The fishermen worked frantically to keep their skiffs afloat while 100-mph winds churned the waters and tested their anchor lines. For several hours, the courageous men rode out the storm, until finally, in the early hours of August 18, the winds subsided. The tide was now unusually low, as the hurricane's winds had pushed a surge of water westward up the Neuse River. Battered but still together, the fishermen debated making a run for the mainland, as they could now put up sail. They knew that this journey of less than ten miles would test their skills. Not all agreed to the plan, but after a few had left, the others soon followed. This proved to be a great mistake. The lull that gave them the opportunity to leave was nothing more than the passing of the hurricane's eye over Swan Island. Within minutes, the storm's winds were again full force, this time gusting from the southwest. The small skiffs were now out on West Bay, and most were capsized by the wind and waves when a ten-foot surge of water washed back from the Neuse River.

Only six of the twenty men who left the island survived. Among those who were rescued were Allen and Almon Hamilton, who saved themselves by quickly taking down their mast and sail, throwing their nets overboard, and lying low in their skiff as it was tossed about. Fourteen others were not as lucky. Of those who drowned, ten were from Sea Level: Joseph and John Lewis, Henry and James Willis, Bart Salter, John Styron, William Salter, John and Joseph Salter, and Micajah Rose. Four brothers from the community of Stacy were lost: John, Kilby, Elijah, and Wallace Smith.

Ocracoke Island was also hard hit by San Ciriaco. The August 21 edition of the *Washington Gazette* reported: "The whole island of Ocracoke is a complete wreck as a result of the fierce storm which swept the entire coast of North Carolina, leaving ruin and disaster in its path. . . . Thirty-three homes were destroyed and two churches were wrecked. Practically every house on the island was damaged to some extent." The article also reported that waves twenty to thirty feet high pounded the beach and that the hurricane's storm tide covered the island with four to five feet of water. Hundreds of banker ponies, sheep, and cows drowned. The dazed survivors of Ocracoke endured "much suffering" after the storm from a lack of food and water.

The residents of Ocracoke and other Outer Banks communities were wise to the effects of rising hurricane tides. Many installed "trap doors" in the floors of their homes to allow rising water to enter, thus preventing the structure from floating off of its foundation and drifting away. Some simply bored holes in the floorboards to relieve the water's pressure. Occasionally, desperate times called for desperate measures. The late Big Ike O'Neal described his adventure in the '99 storm to Associated Press columnist Hal Boyle: "The tides were rising fast and my ole dad, fearful that our house would wash from its foundations, said 'Here son, take this axe and scuttle the floor.' I began chopping away and finally knocked a hole in the floor. Like a big fountain the water gushed in and hit the ceiling and on top of the gusher was a mallard duck that had gotten under our house as the tides pushed upwards."

Hatteras Island was devastated by the August hurricane of '99. The Weather Bureau station in Hatteras Village was hard hit, as the entire southern end of the Outer Banks fell within the powerful right-front quadrant of the storm. Winds at the station were clocked at sustained speeds of over 100 mph, and gusts were measured at between 120 and 140 mph. Ultimately, the station's anemometer was blown away, and no record was made of the storm's highest winds. The barometric pressure was reported as near twenty-six inches, which, if accurate, would suggest that the San Ciriaco hurricane may have reached category-five intensity.

One of the most chilling accounts of the storm was a report filed with the Weather Bureau office in Washington, D.C., by S. L. Doshoz, Weather Bureau observer at Cape Hatteras. The following excerpt from his report details the extent of the storm surge and the struggle for survival endured by the residents of Hatteras Island:

August 21, 1899

This hurricane was, without any question, the most severe of any storm that has ever passed over this section within the memory of any person now living, and there are people here who can remember back for a period of over 75 years. I have made careful inquiry among the old inhabitants here, and they all agree, with one accord, that no storm like this has ever visited the island. Certain it is that no such storm has ever been recorded within the history of the Weather Bureau at this place. The scene here on the 17th was wild and terrifying in the extreme. By 8 A.M. on that date the entire island was covered with water blown in from the sound, and by 11 A.M. all the land was covered to a depth of from 3 to 10 feet. This tide swept over the island at a fearful rate carrying everything movable before it. There were not more than four houses on the island in which the tide did not rise to a depth of from one to four feet, and a least half of the people had to abandon their homes and property to the mercy of the wind and tide and seek the safety of their own lives with those who were fortunate enough to live on higher land.

Language is inadequate to express the conditions which prevailed all day on the 17th. The howling wind, the rushing and roaring tide and the awful sea which swept over the beach and thundered like a thousand pieces of artillery made a picture which was at once appalling and terrible and the like of which Dante's Inferno could scarcely equal. The frightened people were grouped sometimes 40 or 50 in one house, and at times one house would have to be abandoned and they would all have to wade almost beyond their depth in order to reach another. All day this gale, tide and sea continued with a fury and persistent energy that knew no abatement, and the strain on the minds of every one was something so frightful and dejecting that it cannot be expressed. In many houses families were huddled together in the upper portion of the building with the water several feet deep in the lower portion, not knowing what minute the house would either be blown down or swept away by the tide. And even those whose houses were above the water could not tell what minute the tide would rise so high that all dwellings would be swept away.

At about 8 P.M. on the 17th when the wind lulled and shifted to the east and the tide began to run off with great swiftness, causing a fall of several feet in less than a half hour, a prayer of thankfulness went up from every soul on the island, and strong men, who had held up a brave heart against the terrible strain of the past 12 hours, broke down and wept like children upon their minds being relieved of the excessive tension to which it had been subjected all through the day. Cattle, sheep, hogs and chickens were drowned by hundreds before the very eyes of the owners, who were powerless to render any assistance on account of the rushing tide. The fright of these poor animals was terrible to see, and their cries of terror when being surrounded by the water were pitiful in the extreme.

Officer Doshoz also reported on his own personal ordeal and struggle through the hurricane flood:

I live about a mile from the office building and when I went home at 8 A.M., I had to wade in water which was about waist deep. I waited until about 10:30 A.M., thinking the storm would lull, but it did not do so, and at that time I started for the office to change the wind sheet. I got about one-third of the distance and found the water about breast high, when I had to stop in a neighbor's house and rest, the strain of pushing through the water and storm having nearly exhausted my strength. I rested there until about noon when I started again and after going a short distance further I found the water up to my shoulders and still I was not half way to the office. I had to give it up again and take refuge in another neighbor's house where I had to remain until about 8 P.M. when the tide fell so that I could reach the office. I regret that I was unable to change the wind sheet so that a record of the wind could be made from the time the clock stopped running until the [anemometer] cups were blown away, but I did all that I could under the circumstances.

The San Ciriaco hurricane also affected the northern Outer Banks with high winds and storm flooding. At Nags Head, the rising waters of the Atlantic met the wind-driven waters of Albemarle Sound, flooding the entire area, even in places where the beach was one mile wide. Overwash from the storm covered many portions of the Outer Banks, destroying dozens of homes and cottages. Some of the residents of Nags Head refused to leave their homes as the storm approached, as they were confident the rising flood would soon subside. But the water kept coming, and at last some families had to be moved to safety by patrolmen from the Life-Saving Station.

In the nineteenth century, hurricanes were often compared by the number of ships they caused to be wrecked or lost at sea. Powerful storms frequently battered the North Carolina coast and earned the region its nickname: Graveyard of the Atlantic. So many vessels and sailors were lost through the years that young captains were often given special rewards for their first safe passage by the Hatteras coast.

Front Street in Beaufort after the San Ciriaco hurricane of 1899. (Photo courtesy of Charles Aquadro)

The Great Hurricane of '99 scuttled or sank numerous ships from Wilmington to the Virginia line. In his book *Graveyard of the Atlantic*, author David Stick lists seven vessels that were wrecked on the North Carolina coast during the storm: the *Aaron Reppard, Florence Randall, Lydia Willis, Fred Walton, Robert W. Dasey, Priscilla,* and *Minnie Bergen.* Also, the Diamond Shoals Lightship was driven ashore after its mooring lines were broken by the storm's mountainous seas. Six other ships were reported lost at sea without a trace: the *John C. Haynes, M. B. Millen, Albert Schultz, Elwood H. Smith, Henry B. Cleaves,* and *Charles M. Patterson.*

It is known that at least thirty-five sailors from the wrecked vessels were saved as their ships broke apart in the surf. Newspaper accounts concluded that at least thirty lives were lost in these shipwrecks, but the real number of deaths was probably much higher. A newspaper report from Norfolk, Virginia, following the August hurricane described the aftermath: "The stretch of beach between Kinnakeet to Hatteras, a distance of about eighteen miles, bears evidence of the fury of the gale in the shape of spars, masts, and general wreckage of five schooners which were washed ashore and then broken up by the fierce waves, while now and again a body washes ashore to lend added solemnity to the scene."

Of all of this hurricane's wrecks and rescues, one of the most dramatic was that of the barkentine *Priscilla.* This 643-ton American cargo vessel was commanded by Captain Benjamin E. Springsteen and was bound from its home port of Baltimore to Rio de Janeiro, Brazil. When the *Priscilla* left port on August 12, its captain was unaware of the fateful hurricane that would soon meet his ship head-on.

Wreck of the Priscilla *in August 1899. (Photo courtesy of the Outer Banks History Center)*

On the morning of Wednesday, the sixteenth, the wind began to blow, requiring that the ship's light sails be taken in. As the day advanced the winds continued to increase, and orders were given to take in all but the *Priscilla*'s mainsail. But by late afternoon, the driving wind had blown away or destroyed all of the vessel's riggings, and Captain Springsteen was now adrift under bare poles on a rapid southwest course.

Early on the morning of the seventeenth, after a stressful night of rolling seas and hurricane winds, soundings were made to test the water's depth. With each passing hour, the water became more shallow, and the captain knew that the storm was driving his ship ashore. Through the torrents of rain and wind, the order was passed to the crew to prepare to save themselves as the *Priscilla* was about to wreck.

After tossing about for the entire day, the ship finally struck bottom at about 9:00 P.M. on the seventeenth. For the next hour, the *Priscilla* was bashed against the shallow shoals as huge breakers crashed over its hull. Within moments, Captain Springsteen's wife, his son, and two crew members were swept overboard and drowned. Shortly afterward, and with a loud crash, the ship's hull broke apart, and the remaining horrified sailors held tightly to their wreck. Five more terrorizing hours would pass before the captain and his surviving crew would approach the beach.

Even though the hurricane's winds and tide were ferocious, Surfman Rasmus Midgett of the Gull Shoal Life-Saving Station set out on his routine beach patrol at 3:00 A.M. on the eighteenth. The ocean was sweeping completely across the narrow island, at times reaching the saddle girths of his horse.

But Midgett knew that disaster was at hand by the scattered debris that was washed about by the surf. Barrels, crates, buckets, and timbers provided clear signs that a wrecked ship was nearby. Although the night was dark and the storm was intense, this courageous surfman knew that lives were in jeopardy.

Finally, after an hour and a half of treacherous patrol, Midgett stopped on the dark beach at the sound of voices — the distressed cries of the shipwrecked men. Realizing that too much time would be lost if he returned to the station for help, he decided to attempt the rescue alone. One by one, he coaxed the *Priscilla*'s crew off the wreck and into the water, where he helped them to shore through the pounding breakers. Seven men were saved in this manner, and they gathered on the beach, exhausted.

Three of the crew remained on the wreck, however, too bruised and battered to move. Midgett swam out to save them and physically carried them to shore, one at a time. The courageous surfman brought the men to a high dune, where he left them to wait. His coat was offered to Captain Springsteen, who had received a serious wound to the chest. All of the men were bruised and bleeding, and some had their clothes stripped away by the relentless surf.

Midgett quickly returned to his station for help, and several men were dispatched to retrieve the survivors. In all, he had saved ten lives while risking his own in the treacherous waters of the San Ciriaco hurricane. For his efforts, he was later awarded a gold lifesaving medal of honor by the United States secretary of the treasury.

OCTOBER 30–31, 1899

The hurricane that battered the Cape Fear coast on Halloween Day 1899 was the second severe cyclone of the season to strike the Tar Heel state. Residents along the North Carolina coast had come to accept this kind of misfortune; it was the fourth time in less than twenty years that two major hurricanes had hit the state within a single year. Some even speculated that these violent storms were God's punishment to the citizens for allowing dancing on Sundays in local clubs.

The Halloween storm came ashore far to the south of where the San Ciriaco hurricane made landfall in August. And, like Hazel (1954), the Halloween hurricane struck the Brunswick beaches and cut a path through eastern North Carolina into Virginia. Even though the two storms of 1899 crossed different sections of the coast, their widespread effects brought great damage to some of the same locations. With the October hurricane, however, the destruction was most intense in the vicinity of Southport, Wilmington, and Wrightsville Beach.

In the late evening of October 30, the increasing wind and advancing tide offered late warning to the residents of Wrightsville and Carolina Beaches. Be-

cause the beach season had ended, most of the cottages in these resort communities stood empty, except for the caretakers and laborers who serviced them. As the storm rolled through in the early hours of the thirty-first, the greatest damage occurred before daylight. It was much later in the day before the hurricane passed and the people of Wilmington went out to survey the damage. A large crowd boarded the Seacoast train for Wrightsville to witness for themselves the severity of the storm.

When the train rounded the last curve before Wrightsville Station, those on board were not fully prepared for the vast destruction before them. The train screeched to a stop. One reporter from the *Wilmington Messenger* wrote:

> The massive railroad trestle was warped and twisted, and for a few hundred [feet] extending from the station towards the Hammocks the rails and ties were torn from the piles, and presented a tangled wreck piled down in the waters of the sound. The railroad tracks, approaching the station as far toward the city as the Pritchard cottage, was warped and torn and the large platform surrounding the depot was piled high with seaweed and other drift. To the right and left, stretching around the shore of the sound, as far as the eye could reach, where but yesterday, as it were, the famous shell road wound in beautiful curves, was a mass of deep tangled debris of every conceivable kind, the wreckage of cottages from the beach and of boats and bath houses along the shore of the sound.

During the peak of the storm, in many locations the ocean waves broke over the island into Banks Channel, carrying cottages with them. More than twenty cottages were either washed into the sound or completely wrecked by the

The Carolina Yacht Club was heavily damaged in the October hurricane of 1899. The structure was torn down after the storm and then rebuilt using much of the same lumber. (Photo courtesy of the Lower Cape Fear Historical Society)

Oceanfront destruction at Wrightsville Beach, October 1899. (Photo courtesy of the Lower Cape Fear Historical Society)

stormy surf. On the beach the railroad track south of Station Three was washed into Banks Channel, "the cross ties sticking up like a picket fence." Numerous shops, hotels, clubs, and docks were destroyed at Wrightsville. The public pavilion, the Ocean View Hotel, and the old Hewlett barroom were among the losses. The Carolina Yacht Club and the Atlantic Yacht Club were also severely damaged, both having been washed from their foundations and carried by the tides.

Several daring escapes were reported from Wrightsville during the height of the storm. The janitor in charge of the Carolina Club House abandoned the

Wreckage rests on the remains of the railroad tracks at Wrightsville following the 1899 hurricane. (Photo courtesy of the Lower Cape Fear Historical Society)

beach about midnight, before the hurricane reached full intensity. He jumped into a small skiff and sailed to his home in Hewlett's Creek, later describing his ordeal as "terrific in the extreme." Henry Brewington, a watchman for the Ocean View Hotel and several cottages, was forced onto the roof of the Russell cottage by the rising storm surge. When the dwelling collapsed, he swam through the breakers to the Atlantic Club. Realizing that this structure was also doomed, Brewington somehow made his way through the tide and back to the trestle at Wrightsville Station. J. T. Dooley, a railroad employee who lived on the Hammocks, narrowly escaped the rising waters with his wife and three children. At 3:30 A.M. he crossed the railway bridge with his family, and at 4:00 A.M. the trestle was destroyed by the pounding surf.

The destruction at Carolina Beach was equal to that of Wrightsville. The railroad tracks were damaged, numerous cottages were destroyed or "missing," and reports indicated that waves rolled through the town. Along the Wilmington waterfront, the Cape Fear River flooded the wharves from one end of the city to the other. Here, the water did not reach its high mark until 9:00 A.M., and then it fell rapidly. The flooding damaged stored goods all along the waterfront. As the waters rose inside the Atlantic and Yadkin Warehouse, a large quantity of lime became wet, causing fires to break out. The local fire department was called in to extinguish the flames. Somehow, a large flat of bricks was carried into the river by the storm, and "no trace of it has been found." It was also reported that "driftwood of every description, and seaweed were brought up the river in thick processions covering the entire surface of the river in some locations."

On the afternoon of October 31, a large trunk was found drifting in the river near the Wilmington docks. Inside were clothes, coins, and papers belonging to J. W. Brock. Because Brock was known to have been fishing at Zeke's Island prior to the storm, there was speculation that his fishing party was washed away when the island was "completely covered" by the hurricane's surge. Brock was never heard from.

The damage at Southport caused one resident to report: "The storm here was the worst ever known and great damage was done." The storm tide rose five feet above normal high water, and many houses along the waterfront were badly damaged. The Norwegian bark *Johannah* was being "disinfected" at the Cape Fear quarantine station when the storm approached. The entire quarantine crew took refuge on the ship, which broke anchor and washed aground up the river. The Southport waterfront was littered with the wreckage of the hurricane, including numerous small boats, the remains of the city wharves, and the passenger steamer *Southport*. According to the *Messenger*, "Large droves of cattle drifted across the river, dead and alive. They were run off by high waters all over Bald Head Island, which never was known to be covered before."

The hurricane struck north of the Cape Fear region as well. The New River Inn and over a dozen cottages were swept away in Onslow County. One report claimed that all the oysters in New River were covered by sand deposited by the tides, and none could be harvested for years. Also, Old Stump Inlet, said to have been closed for more than a generation, was reopened by this storm and was reported to have had twelve feet of water on its bar.

Farther up the coast in Morehead City and Beaufort, the effects of the Halloween hurricane were as unwelcomed as the tragedies that had struck with the San Ciriaco storm. High water again flooded the low-lying reaches of these coastal towns. In New Bern, the storm brought that city "the worst experience in her history." The water was two feet higher than during the August hurricane, and once again fires caused by wet lime broke out on the docks. Few reports were offered from other coastal villages, such as Portsmouth and Ocracoke, but the Halloween hurricane was likely to have been felt along much of the Carolina coast.

HURRICANES OF THE NEW CENTURY,
1900–1950

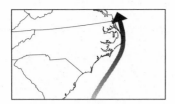

NOVEMBER 13, 1904

The first severe hurricane of the twentieth century to move across the North Carolina coast came late in 1904, on November 13. This category-three storm passed near Hatteras during the morning and brought high tides and heavy rains to the entire coast. Two schooners were wrecked near Cape Fear, and extensive damage was reported at Fort Caswell. At New Inlet, the storm surge swept away the Life-Saving Station, and four crewmen drowned. Four more lives were lost in the wreck of the *Missouri*, a schooner that went down near Washington, North Carolina. Several lives were lost when a fishing lodge on Hatteras Island was swept away by the tides, and eight more people drowned when a yacht sank in Pamlico Sound. As the hurricane moved past the coast, a large cold-air mass was drawn into the cyclone's circulation, and an early snow fell across much of the state.

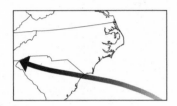

SEPTEMBER 17, 1906

On September 17, 1906, a severe hurricane made landfall near Myrtle Beach and caused considerable damage along the southern coast. Although the winds in Wilmington reached only 50 mph, the tides were high and breakers were reported in the streets of Wrightsville Beach. Just as in the Halloween hurricane of 1899, the trolley car trestle to Wrightsville was damaged. Several cottages and a hotel were washed away, and more than two hundred people were rescued by boat. One unusual account from this storm came from Masonboro, where Walter Parsley reported finding large bowling balls in his front yard after the storm. Although the balls were made from a dense wood called *lignum vitae*, they had somehow washed across the sound from Wrightsville.

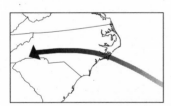

SEPTEMBER 3, 1913

On the morning of September 3, 1913, a short-lived but severe hurricane crossed over Core Banks into Pamlico Sound. It decreased in intensity as it continued on a west-northwest path, passing south of Raleigh in the afternoon. Although its fury could not be compared with the "great" hurricanes, this storm brought surprising amounts of floodwaters and destruction to several down-east locations. A maximum wind velocity of 74 mph was reported at Cape Hatteras, but this storm's greatest impact occurred when the wind-driven waters of Pamlico Sound were pushed inland.

The most severe flooding was reported in New Bern and Washington. The streets of New Bern were inundated by the overflowing Neuse River, which reached a new record level for that location: nine feet above normal high water. A large railroad bridge that spanned the Neuse was washed away, and

The Washington, N.C., waterfront after the destructive flood of 1913.
(Photo courtesy of the George H. and Laura E. Brown Library)

New Bern residents look over the water and debris filling Johnson Street after the September hurricane of 1913. (Photo courtesy of the North Carolina Maritime Museum)

damage to homes and businesses was extensive. Crop damage was significant throughout the region.

In Washington, the water rose ten feet above normal, and the flooding extended all the way to Third Street, which is the fourth street from the river. There was so much water on Main Street that "speed boats were coming and going" most of the following day. The Norfolk and Southern trestle, the Washington and Vandemere trestle, and the old county bridge were all washed away and had to be rebuilt the year following the storm.

As in past hurricanes, several ships were reported as wrecked or lost. These included the *Dewey*, which sank at Cape Lookout, the schooners *Manteo* and *Grace G. Bennett*, which became stranded near Portsmouth, and the Boston schooner *George W. Wells*, which wrecked about five hundred yards offshore at Ocracoke. At 317 feet and almost three thousand tons, the *Wells* was hailed as the largest sailing vessel of its kind in the world. In a terrifying fourteen-hour ordeal, the passengers and crew of the *Wells* were saved by the courageous men of the Hatteras Inlet Life-Saving Station.

The hurricane of 1913 may have been only a category-one storm, but its westerly movement through Pamlico Sound and across the state brought great destruction to a broad area. Crops were damaged and structures were destroyed throughout eastern North Carolina. At Goldsboro, the storm was "the worst in history," and similar reports came from Tarboro, Wilson, Farmville, and Durham. In all, five lives were lost and property damage was estimated at $3 million.

JULY 14–16, 1916

Although the midsummer hurricane of 1916 actually moved ashore on the South Carolina coast, its northwest movement carried it inland through the North Carolina mountains on July 15. There the storm dumped record amounts of rain across the southern Appalachians. The heaviest rains were recorded at Altapass, where 22.22 inches fell during the twenty-four-hour period ending at 2:00 P.M. on the sixteenth. This downpour established a new twenty-four-hour rainfall record for the entire United States.

Winds from the storm were less than hurricane strength in North Carolina, but the deluge of rain brought deadly landslides to the mountain countryside. Bridges and highways were washed away, and crops suffered great damage. Railroads were undermined in numerous locations, shutting down the lifelines of rail transport. Several persons were killed in the mudslides that followed the record rains. No significant damage occurred along the North Carolina coast.

SEPTEMBER 18–19, 1928

The Great Hurricane of 1928 brought epic destruction to Puerto Rico and Florida before it tracked northward through the Carolinas. On September 13, the hurricane moved over Puerto Rico, where winds were clocked at 160 mph and 300 lives were lost. As the great storm moved over eastern Florida on the seventeenth, the wind-driven waters of Lake Okeechobee overflowed into populated areas, causing a massive flood. In Florida, 1,836 were killed, mostly due to drowning.

By the time the hurricane crossed into the sandhills of North Carolina on the night of September 18, its destructive winds had diminished, but tremendous rains fell across the Tar Heel state. The resulting floods were very severe and the highest on record for some upper portions of the Cape Fear River. At Fayetteville, where the bank-full stage is 35 feet, the river reached an unprecedented height of 64.7 feet. At Elizabethtown, the river rose to 41.3 feet. Flooding at Lumberton was reported as "the worst in history," and thousands of acres of crop lands were underwater. Many highways were closed because of bridge washouts and deep-standing water.

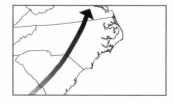

OCTOBER 1–2, 1929

Another major hurricane struck Florida and tracked northward through the Carolinas in 1929. Like the storm of the previous year, the 1929 hurricane lost much of its wind energy before it reached the south-central region of North Carolina. But the storm's massive rain clouds emptied as it crossed the state,

Oceanfront cottages at Wrightsville Beach were left exposed following the October hurricane of 1929. (Photo courtesy of the New Hanover County Public Library)

again causing severe river flooding and crop damage. Record rainfall amounts were reported in many locations. Flooding on the Cape Fear was very near the record level of the previous year, and at one station near Fayetteville the river rose forty-one feet in one twenty-four-hour period. For the second straight year, many portions of North Carolina "foundered in flood."

AUGUST 22–23, 1933

By 1932, the Great Depression had a firm grip on the nation and had cast its long shadow across North Carolina. Times were hard from the Appalachians to the coastal plains. In November of that year, Franklin D. Roosevelt was elected president with the promise of a New Deal for economic recovery. By the summer of 1933, there seemed to be reasonable hope among the people of the nation. But for many coastal North Carolinians, the months of August and September would bring a far greater despair than the recent economic turmoil.

Once again North Carolina was struck by two hurricanes within a single season. On August 22 and again on September 15, the coastal region was awash with storms. The August hurricane, ranked as a category two in intensity, passed over the northern Outer Banks, and in September a deadly category-three hurricane spun through Pamlico Sound and up the coast.

The first of the two storms passed east of Ocracoke just after midnight on the morning of August 23. By midmorning, the hurricane was on a curving

The August hurricane of 1933 caused significant soundside destruction at Nags Head. (Photo courtesy of the Outer Banks History Center, Wise Family Collection)

path back toward the Atlantic by way of Norfolk, Virginia. At Cape Hatteras, the maximum winds were only 64 mph. But high tides and severe beach erosion were reported all along the banks. Crops were damaged as far inland as Granville County, and Norfolk, Virginia, was flooded by "several feet" of water. In the northeastern counties, the damage was estimated at $250,000.

SEPTEMBER 15–16, 1933

Less than one month after the August storm, another hurricane moved toward the coast. By the morning of September 15, it had reached a position 250 miles south of Cape Hatteras, and all indications were that it would cross the North Carolina coastline late that night or early the next morning. Storm warnings were issued, and the few coastal cities that had hurricane plans put them into effect. The American Red Cross, better organized after its recent experience with tragic hurricanes in Florida, urged the Carolina chapters to prepare for a potential disaster.

When the hurricane approached the mainland, it swerved to the north. As it pushed through Pamlico Sound, intense northeast winds forced tremendous quantities of water to surge to the southwest, flooding the river basins of the Neuse and the Pamlico. An unusual phenomenon occurred along the northern banks of the Albemarle Sound when the water was "blown away" to the lowest level ever recorded for that region.

The tremendous storm tide that swept through several down-east communities claimed twenty-one lives and left extensive destruction. The wind-driven water remained high on the land until the storm moved up the coast.

Then, like a cork removed from a bathtub, the water rushed back toward the sea, overwashing Core Banks from west to east and opening Drum Inlet in the process. Winds were recorded at 92 mph at Cape Hatteras, just before the anemometer was destroyed. In Beaufort and New Bern, winds were estimated at up to 125 mph. In some areas, wind-related damage was as severe as the flooding. Countless large trees were downed throughout the east, including the city of New Bern. In an article from the *New York Times*, a reporter wrote: "New Bern has long been known as the 'Athens of North Carolina' because of its many large and beautiful trees. Now hundreds of these trees are either lying in the streets or leaning grotesquely against the battered houses. Many of the splendid trees of East Front, Broad, Pollock, Johnson, and Craven streets were blown down."

The flooding in New Bern was the highest ever known and was said to have been about two feet greater than in the storm tide of September 1913. The water reached a height of three to four feet in some streets, and rowboats and skiffs were used to evacuate people from buildings that were completely surrounded by water. The tide rose a foot above the tallest piling on the Coast Guard dock, and the dock was wrecked and washed away. The cutter *Pamlico* was unharmed, however, even though it was moored to the dock at the time.

The Neuse River bridge that linked New Bern and Bridgeton on U.S. 17 was washed out at about 1:30 A.M. on September 16. A three-quarter-mile-long section was taken out by the surging waters of the Neuse, and pieces of the bridge were scattered along the shore for miles downriver. Two stalled automobiles were believed to have been stranded on this section, but their occupants were able to escape the bridge before it collapsed. Damage was also reported to the Norfolk and Southern railroad trestle and the Trent River bridge. Several boxcars were dumped into the Neuse when the Atlantic Coastline pier caved in.

One unusual story from the "storm of '33" came from the New Bern area. The roof of Mrs. Sam Smallwood's boathouse was blown off by the fierce winds. It landed, right side up, on a seawall a quarter mile downriver, with Mrs. Smallwood's boat, which had been suspended from the rafters, still intact. The boat was retrieved the morning of the storm and was used to take Mrs. Smallwood to higher ground.

The damage in New Bern alone was more than $1 million. Many homes and businesses were severely damaged by both high water and winds. Several lumber factories were severely damaged. The rising tides of salt water reached the region's farmlands, and damage was heavy to unharvested corn, cotton, and sweet potatoes. In many locations, tons of tobacco stored in barns were destroyed when they became soaked by heavy rains and rising floodwaters. But by far, the greatest loss and suffering came to those who lived near the water and made their living from the sea. Carteret County was hit hard by the storm, and remote communities down east were devastated.

Few photographs exist to document the great destruction left in the wake of the September 1933 hurricane. Some of the hardest hit areas were the down-east villages of Carteret County, where few residents had cameras. The effects of the storm's 125-mph winds can be seen in this image of a machine shop in Morehead City. (Photo courtesy of H. S. Gibbs Jr.)

The *Beaufort News* reported the following events the week following the storm:

The oldest citizens here in Beaufort have told the News that it was the most devastating storm that they have seen in the past four score years. It was not merely a bad wind that reached gale force for just a few minutes; the disastrous hurricane swept Carteret for more than twelve hours without ceasing for even a few minutes. From early Friday morning rain began falling and this continued unremittingly until about day break Saturday morning.

This terrific tropical hurricane which swept up the Atlantic coast Friday seemed to have hit Carteret near Beaufort Inlet, striking Beaufort and Morehead City first, then continued with its destructive force on to Merrimon, South River, Lukens, Roe and Lola, with all other communities in eastern Carteret getting their shares of the devastating tempest. . . . Within Carteret County alone there was a property loss of at least a million dollars, eight people were drowned and scores left homeless, hundreds without food and more with barely enough clothing to cover their bodies. Thousands of domestic and wild animals perished in the water and if they are not removed and buried decomposition will result in stench and disease. In the villages where homes and other buildings were wholly or partially demolished, men, women and children by the score stuck nails in their feet and have cuts and bruises and sprains across their bodies. Only a very small percentage have received medical attention and been inoculated with tetanus antitoxin. Sanitary conditions in the stricken area are terrible, and epidemics will in all likelihood ensue if the people do not cooperate whole-heartedly with the sanitary engineers of the State Department of Health.

Captain Jim Hamilton and his three sons, Nelson, Charlie, and Ralph, all drowned in Long Bay when their twenty-foot skiff capsized in the storm. Like countless other fishermen before them, they had left their home in Sea Level with no knowledge of the impending weather. Their expedition quickly turned tragic as their small boat was no match for the furious seas.

In the down-east community of Merrimon, the tide was estimated at "fif-teen or sixteen feet." Only four out of thirty houses remained after the tides overwashed the area. The Carraway family endured a horrible ordeal when their house collapsed during the storm. The entire family huddled together as a blast of wind tore down the structure, pinning them in the wreckage and the rising tides. Mr. Carraway escaped with the help of his son George, but Freda Carraway remained trapped under the debris. Those who escaped were forced to flee to higher ground when the tides continued to rise, but Freda remained trapped under the house, where she apparently drowned.

At nearby Cedar Island, about eight families endured the hurricane, and al-most all of their homes were washed off their foundations or severely dam-aged. In his book *Sailin' with Grandpa*, author Sonny Williamson offers a detailed account of the scene as recorded by Captain John Day and his wife, Adelaide. Day had come to Cedar Island by boat to check on his relatives in the remote community. Virtually every structure suffered damage in the storm, and the bewildered residents struggled to simply survive in the first days following their ordeal.

After the hurricane passed, the local director of the Red Cross, Frank Hyde, launched a relief mission for the down-east villages. No communication was possible with the isolated hurricane victims, and this voyage would provide the first news of the conditions in these areas. Thirty "orders" of food and supplies were prepared for the relief effort, which was assisted by the Coast Guard. Hyde left Fort Macon for Core Sound early Monday morning, two days after the hurricane's arrival.

The mission reached Lola, on the southern end of Cedar Island, by late morning. James Whitehurst, reporter for the *Beaufort News*, was traveling with Dr. Hyde and filed the following report:

Upon arriving on shore we were conducted through a throng of half-clothed bewildered people who looked upon us with overjoyed eyes. One young woman with a baby—it appeared to be her first—cried with joy. Every person seemed to have stuck nails in their feet or had cuts and bruis-es about their bodies. The last food in Lola had been consumed for break-fast, and this had been far from sufficient.

The homes had been washed from their foundations, windows had been blown out, roofs and roofing wrenched from the tops of the structures. Wreckage was strewn from one end of the island to the other. Few of the people had shoes on, and virtually every one had on all the clothing they had been able to salvage.

When the Coast Guard boat carrying Dr. Hyde moved to the northern end of the island, its passengers found even greater destruction in the village of Roe. Eight or ten homes were described as totally destroyed, and only one was "fit for winter." Most of the homes had floated haphazardly with the tides, and many suffered structural damage. Thick mattes of mud, grass, and debris filled several houses and littered the branches of nearby trees.

At South River, similar floods struck late Friday night. The Louis Cannon family narrowly escaped drowning when their home collapsed in the storm. They had gathered in their attic when the waters rushed into the first floor. They eventually escaped by clinging to the rooftop of the broken house until they became caught in the top of a grove of trees. There they rode out the storm until the waters receded.

The home of William Cannon became a refuge for other South River residents who were forced to flee their homes. The Cannon residence was on higher ground than many other houses, and frightened neighbors and relatives made their way there when the floods moved in. Ultimately, more than fifty people were sheltered in this one house. Many stayed through Saturday, until they were able to return to what was left of their homes.

One of the great tragedies of the '33 storm struck the family of Elijah Dixon, who were staying in a two-story home near Back Creek when the hurricane hit. Dixon, his wife Ellen, their eight-year-old daughter Hazel, three-year-old son James, and nine-month-old daughter Elva Marie were all plunged into the raging waters when the house washed into Back Creek. The family tried desperately to cling to the broken fragments of the rooftop. With his young son around his neck, Dixon jumped into the dark waters to rescue his wife, who was still clinging onto baby Elva. In the darkness and confusion, the infant slipped from her arms and drowned. As the weary group again gathered on the roof, they realized that young Hazel was also missing. Reeling from this double tragedy, Dixon still managed to grasp a large branch when the rooftop was swept into a grove of trees. There the battered family remained until later Saturday afternoon, when they were rescued.

The tragedies of the 1933 hurricane were spread throughout numerous down-east communities. At Oriental, Vandemere, Bayboro, and Arapahoe, local newspapers reported that "hardly a building was left intact." From Ocracoke, there was a report that "four feet of water had covered the island."

As the hurricane's storm surge pushed over Ocracoke, residents scrambled for high ground in any way they could. Some had prepared their homes by removing floorboards to prevent the tides from washing their houses "off the blocks." Many rode out the hurricane in their attics, and some were forced onto their rooftops.

At the Green Island Hunt Club, on the eastern end of Ocracoke, nine people took refuge as the storm approached. The two-story clubhouse was rocked by pounding surf, and by midnight, "the ocean was breaking in the kitchen." As the first floor filled with water, the occupants gathered on the second floor, which also began to flood. Like so many other storm victims throughout the region, the group was forced to crawl through a high window onto the roof, where they rode out the storm. The structure pitched and rolled like a boat, and the constant up and down motion washed away the foundation, digging a deep hole in the sand. The frightened men and women held desperately to the rooftop through the gusting winds and strong surf until, at daybreak, the storm passed.

As the tides receded, the survivors climbed down off the clubhouse. To their amazement, the wave action had dug the house so far down that the second-floor windows were level with the ground. The fishermen were also surprised to see their boats cast upon a nearby beach. During the storm, these small craft were blown out into the sound, but when the hurricane passed and the winds shifted, they were blown right back, suffering little damage.

The September hurricane of 1933 left many scars on the North Carolina coast. In all, twenty-one were dead and damage estimates topped $3 million. The Red Cross estimated the area of greatest suffering to be a nine-county region with a population of 120,000. Their survey indicated that 1,166 buildings had been totally destroyed and 7,244 severely damaged. The Red Cross gave aid to 1,281 families, many of whom received help with the rebuilding of their homes. This effort helped temper the anguish from one of the most tragic storms in North Carolina history.

SEPTEMBER 18, 1936

The residents of North Carolina's Outer Banks suffered through another severe hurricane on September 18, 1936. Like so many storms, this hurricane swept along the banks with its eye just offshore, curving back out to sea before its intense eastern half could reach land. Even though the eye remained over the ocean, the hurricane was quite severe, especially along the northern coast. Winds of 90 mph were reported at Manteo, and Hatteras station recorded an average five-minute wind speed of 80 mph.

The strong northeast winds brought significant beach erosion to the coast. About thirty-five feet of beach were lost at Nags Head. Many roads and highways were covered with water and sand, and bridges were undercut by the

Many of Southport's riverfront docks and shrimp houses were destroyed in the August hurricane of 1944. (Photo courtesy of Leila H. Pigott)

tides. The highway from Currituck to Norfolk was washed out, hampering relief efforts after the storm.

On Hatteras Island, residents once again had to reckon with the "hoigh toide on the sound soide." Rising water washed numerous homes off their foundations. Some families opened their doors to the storm, allowing flood-waters to wash through their houses, thus preventing the structures from being swept away. After the tides receded, brooms were used to sweep out the heavy silt that had collected on the floors and baseboards.

The Hatteras residents were threatened by disease after the '36 hurricane, and drinking water was scarce. Large cisterns used to collect rainwater were contaminated after the storm, and each one had to be disinfected with bleach. Outdoor toilets were common, and most had overflowed in the flood, contaminating the drinking water and presenting the threat of disease. Typhoid vaccine was administered by a local doctor to most residents. Until the cisterns could be cleaned and more rains could come, many of the people living on the island had no water to drink. Fortunately, the American Red Cross brought in drinking water for a period of weeks after the storm.

The 1936 hurricane was severe from Cape Hatteras through southern Virginia. But fortunately, this storm was not as destructive (it ranks as a category two) as it might have been had it continued on its northwest track. Nevertheless, it still caused $1.6 million in damages in North Carolina and Virginia and claimed two lives.

AUGUST 1, 1944

The 1944 hurricane season was active along the East Coast, and North Carolina felt the effects of two hurricanes that year. The first was a storm of small diameter that moved northward past the Bahamas on July 30 and made landfall near Southport at about 8:00 P.M. on August 1. This category-one hurricane brought winds of 80 mph to Oak Island, and gusts in Wilmington reached 72 mph. The greatest reports of damage came from Carolina Beach, although the waterfront in Southport suffered severely.

A remarkable evacuation of island residents and vacationers was completed at Wrightsville and Carolina Beaches. It was estimated that ten thousand people were removed from these resorts, and many were taken out in the desperate hours of the storm's arrival. One hundred army trucks were brought in from nearby Camp Davis to assist with the transport as army, Coast Guard, and police officers went door to door calling for residents to leave. Many vacationers attempted to flee in their cars and were trapped in rising waters that stalled their vehicles. The Wrightsville Causeway and Carolina Beach road were flooded, and stalled cars blocked the transport of evacuees. Soldiers and police worked quickly to push aside the cars and successfully complete the evacuation.

During the peak of the storm, a two-and-a-half-ton amphibious vehicle was called in from Camp Davis to rescue seven stranded soldiers from Hogshead Island in the Cape Fear River. The "duck" was driven into the river through towering waves and reached the island within a few minutes. The soldiers, stationed at nearby Fort Fisher, would likely have drowned had they not been rescued, according to their commanding officer.

Although it is possible the winds never reached 100 mph, trees and power lines were downed throughout the region. Large plate-glass windows were blown out in downtown Wilmington, and some of the city's most majestic oaks were toppled. No deaths were reported, but there were several injuries, including two young boys who were burned by downed power lines. A local paper boldly reported that this was "the greatest storm to strike here in the past 200 years."

The most extensive damage occurred at Carolina Beach. Thirty-foot waves reportedly pounded the beachfront and totally destroyed the town's famed boardwalk. According to the *Wilmington Morning Star*, oceanfront homes were washed from their foundations, which "left them at crazy tilts like the hats of drunken sailors weaving down the street." At Wrightsville, the greatest damage occurred to the new sewage project, which was under construction and was left completely covered by sand. Police officers who remained at Wrightsville through the storm reported that "at one time, the water measured 18 feet by the City Hall." The total damage from the storm exceeded $2 million.

SEPTEMBER 14, 1944

The second hurricane of 1944 to strike North Carolina brought death and destruction to nine hundred miles of coastline from Cape Hatteras to Newfoundland. The Great Atlantic Hurricane of 1944 approached the Outer Banks on the morning of September 14 and passed just east of Cape Hatteras on a track toward New England. The eye of the hurricane remained offshore, and North Carolina's coast was spared a direct hit. But as the great storm moved northward, its forward speed increased, and it slammed into Long Island, New York, at about 10:00 P.M. the same day. The damage was heavy in New York, Connecticut, Rhode Island, Massachusetts, and Maine.

The pattern and destruction of the '44 storm was very similar to that of the Great New England Hurricane of 1938. The '38 storm still ranks as one of our nation's worst natural disasters. The American Red Cross reported that it claimed 494 lives (more than another 100 were lost at sea), destroyed over four thousand homes and buildings, and brought $350 million in damages to the northeastern states. Although the 1938 hurricane brought no serious effects to North Carolina, it did blow by Hatteras and then accelerate to the north, reaching an incredible forward speed of 56 mph. This meteoric movement intensified the storm's effects on the New England coastline, and the hurricane's surge drowned scores of coastal residents. During the 1938 hurricane, one of the highest wind speeds in U.S. history was recorded in Milton, Massachusetts—a gust measuring 186 mph.

Most of the homes and businesses destroyed by the Great New England Hurricane of 1938 had been rebuilt by the summer of 1944. But the Great Atlantic Storm of '44 again flooded the northeast, and damage from this hurricane was heavy. In North Carolina, the '44 storm was called the "worst ever" by some on the Outer Banks, who again watched as the ocean and sound met, surrounding their homes with water. On Ocracoke, the tide rose two to four feet in many houses. As they had done so many times in the past, residents there opened their doors to the rising waters to keep their homes in place. Fish were reportedly trapped under furniture and left behind when the storm passed and the waters receded.

The hurricane moved northward up the banks at about 30 mph on the morning of September 14. At Cape Hatteras, the weather station recorded a barometric pressure reading of 27.97 inches, the lowest to date for that location. Even though its center remained at sea, the storm's massive eye wobbled up Hatteras Island and was discernible to the island's residents. It was reported that the eye was so large that many had time to leave their homes to check on their boats, visit friends, and survey the damages in the area. Some were caught off guard when the hurricane's eye passed by and winds exceeding 100 mph "hauled around," blowing from the northwest.

During the storm's approach, strong southeast winds had filled the sounds with ocean water, backing up all the rivers, creeks, and marshes on the mainland side. Some on Hatteras Island reported that the winds had blown the waters so far west that the sound was left dry for nearly a mile. But as the eye passed and the winds turned around, the waters of Pamlico and Albemarle Sounds rushed back toward the banks, flooding villages from Hatteras to Nags Head. Time and again this phenomenon of wind and water recurs with passing hurricanes, each time bringing new potential to reshape the Outer Banks.

The most serious flooding was in Avon. During the 1930s, the Civilian Conservation Corps had installed miles of fencing on the beach, which collected sand to form a protective barrier. The "sand walls" practically surrounded the town. When the '44 hurricane's west winds pushed the sound into the village, the sand walls became a dike that prevented the waters from escaping. The massive surge could not continue on across the bank to the ocean, and Avon became a deep pool. Residents reported seeing cars and trucks completely covered by the tides. Houses drifted about, sometimes crashing into each other. One young girl, huddled in desperation with her family in a second-story hallway, actually became seasick as her home was sloshed about by the tide and wind. Avon was hit hard, as 96 of the town's 115 houses were severely damaged or washed off their foundations.

Along the northern banks, the pounding northeast winds and waves scoured out the skeletons of forgotten shipwrecks, some of which had been buried for generations. There was heavy damage in Elizabeth City and in the Nags Head area, some from flooding but much from the storm's high winds. At Cape Hatteras, winds were estimated at 110 mph (after the anemometer failed), but at Cape Henry, Virginia, the hurricane's top speed was recorded at 134 mph. The highest gust at that location was estimated at 150 mph. Maximum wind velocities equaled or exceeded all previous records at Hatteras, Cape Henry, Atlantic City, New Jersey, New York City, and Block Island, Rhode Island.

Although only one North Carolinian was killed in the Great Atlantic Hurricane of 1944, the storm was deadly overall. In the northeast, 45 more lives were lost, including 26 in Massachusetts. But most tragically, 344 more people died at sea as five ships sank during the hurricane. Two of those were lost off of the North Carolina coast. The Coast Guard cutters *Jackson* and *Bedloe* both capsized and sank while guarding a liberty ship that had been torpedoed near Cape Hatteras. German U-boats were active at that time in attacking allied vessels that moved along the Outer Banks. The '44 hurricane provided only a brief interruption in their acts of war.

HURRICANE ALLEY,
1950–1960

During the fifties, while most of America was laughing at Milton Berle, rockin' with Elvis, or worrying about Khrushchev and the bomb, the people of eastern North Carolina were grappling with a different kind of surprise attack —hurricanes. Throughout history these violent storms had visited the Carolina coastline with random frequency. Sometimes they had struck twice or even three times within a single year. Most often, however, several years had passed between major storms, and coastal residents had been able to pick up the pieces of their lives and rebuild before the next hurricane. But for a period in the mid-1950s, a flurry of hurricane activity dispelled all statistical expectations. Seven hurricanes blasted the Tar Heel state in roughly two years, leaving death and great destruction in their wake. Included in this group was the most infamous of all North Carolina hurricanes, the "lady" known as Hazel. The great destruction brought on by this group of storms earned a new nickname for the region: Hurricane Alley.

BARBARA (AUGUST 13, 1953)

In 1953 the United States Weather Bureau officially began providing women's names for hurricanes in the Atlantic. Hurricane Barbara, the second-named storm of that season, struck the coast of North Carolina between Morehead City and Ocracoke on August 13. After spinning northward along the Outer Banks, the storm turned to the northeast and moved out to sea near the Virginia line. Barbara was a category-one hurricane, and damages were not severe. The storm's highest winds were reported as gusts to 90 mph at Cape Hatteras and Nags Head. Several locations along the coast reported rainfall exceeding six inches, but winds and rains on the mainland were very light. Damage estimates exceeded $1 million, but most of this was attributed to crop damage. The only death associated with Barbara occurred at Wrightsville Beach, where a man was swept from a pier and drowned.

CAROL (AUGUST 30, 1954)

One year later, on August 30, 1954, hurricane Carol accelerated up the Atlantic coast, just missing Cape Hatteras. The hurricane's eye passed the cape at about 10:00 P.M. on a north-northeast track. Because the Outer Banks remained on the storm's weaker western side, damages were not severe. Beach erosion was significant, and some homes and fishing piers were damaged. About one thousand feet of highway were undermined on the banks. Although property damage at any given locality was light, damage spread along the coast totaled $250,000. Carol's highest winds were between 90 and 100 mph at Cape Hatteras. Gusts were recorded to 65 mph at Cherry Point and 55 mph at Wilmington. Tides ran from three to five feet above normal.

Residents of the coastal Carolinas faced the recurring ordeal of hurricanes for an extended period during the 1950s. (Photo courtesy of the News and Observer Publishing Co./N.C. Division of Archives and History)

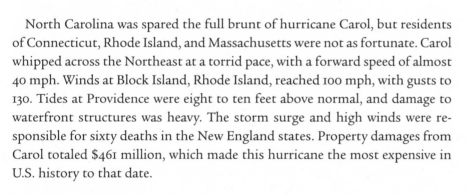

Homeowners and merchants whose properties faced the ocean suffered the greatest losses from the hurricanes of the 1950s. (Photo courtesy of the News and Observer Publishing Co./N.C. Division of Archives and History)

North Carolina was spared the full brunt of hurricane Carol, but residents of Connecticut, Rhode Island, and Massachusetts were not as fortunate. Carol whipped across the Northeast at a torrid pace, with a forward speed of almost 40 mph. Winds at Block Island, Rhode Island, reached 100 mph, with gusts to 130. Tides at Providence were eight to ten feet above normal, and damage to waterfront structures was heavy. The storm surge and high winds were responsible for sixty deaths in the New England states. Property damages from Carol totaled $461 million, which made this hurricane the most expensive in U.S. history to that date.

EDNA (SEPTEMBER 10, 1954)

Less than two weeks after Carol had passed, residents along the North Carolina coast were told that another hurricane was headed their way. Hurricane Edna followed a track very similar to that of Carol, sweeping past the Bahama Islands and curving northward toward the Tar Heel coast. Fortunately, Edna also passed offshore, missing Cape Hatteras by some sixty miles.

Once again, damages were generally light but widespread along the Outer

A sense of bewilderment came over many who searched for the remains of their homes at Long Beach following hurricane Hazel in October 1954. (Photo courtesy of Lewis J. Hardee)

Banks. Television aerials, roofs, and fishing piers were damaged from Ocracoke to the Virginia line. Another section of highway was washed out on Hatteras Island. Beach erosion was severe in some areas due to large waves and strong currents brought on by northeast winds that gusted to 75 mph.

But like Carol, hurricane Edna missed the North Carolina coast and sped northward to strike the northeastern states. Edna made landfall near the eastern tip of Long Island, New York, on September 11. Winds gusted to 120 mph at Martha's Vineyard, Massachusetts, and a great storm tide again flooded the region. The death toll from this storm reached twenty-one and damages exceeded $40 million. Edna landed a knockout punch to numerous coastal communities that were still reeling from the devastation left by hurricane Carol. The 1954 hurricane season turned out to be one of the most destructive in New England history.

HAZEL (OCTOBER 15, 1954)

Carol and Edna had given the residents of coastal North Carolina a brief scare and a taste of nasty weather. But as it turned out, these two storms were only warning shots fired beyond the coastline. The next hurricane took dead aim on Brunswick County and would eventually be recognized as the greatest natural disaster to ever affect the state. Its name was Hazel.

Hazel began, like many other hurricanes, as a trough of low pressure over the warm waters of the tropical Atlantic Ocean. On October 5, 1954, the small storm was identified just east of Grenada and was observed on a west-northwest track that would take it through the Grenadines. Winds were clocked at 95 mph, and the small island of Carriacou was the first to suffer from Hazel's winds and tides.

At the Weather Bureau's Miami office, chief forecaster Grady Norton was working twelve-hour days plotting Hazel's course. Tragically, Norton suffered a stroke on the morning of October 9 and died later the same day. The Weather Bureau scrambled to pick up where Norton had left off, following the daily reports of the growing storm. Although he had been warned by his doctor to avoid the long hours, Norton had ignored his medical condition out of concern for the hurricane's potential for destruction.

Hazel continued to draw energy from the warm Caribbean waters and intensified as it curved northward toward Haiti. During the early morning hours of October 12, the well-organized storm slammed into the Haitian coast, raking over both the southern and northern peninsulas.

Haiti was devastated. Several small towns were "almost totally demolished," and larger cities such as Jeremie and Port de Paix suffered severe wind damage. Torrential rains fell over the island nation, flooding rivers, washing out roads and bridges, and filling homes and businesses with mud. Heavy rains caused a massive landslide that buried the mountain village of Berley, killing almost all of its 260 residents. Winds in excess of 125 mph were reported from several Haitian cities. Tides reached record levels on the southern peninsula, and surge flooding was extreme. It was estimated that as many as one thousand Haitians may have died in the storm.

As Hazel moved through the Windward Passage on the morning of October 13, observers noticed that its winds had diminished to a mere 40 mph. This low wind speed was the result of a distortion of the hurricane as it passed over the mountainous Haitian terrain. But Hazel rapidly regained its strength and form over the next few hours. After passing the Bahamas, it was again a major cyclone, and all warning messages issued for the United States coast indicated sustained winds in excess of 100 mph.

The eye of the hurricane passed about ninety-five miles east of Charleston, South Carolina, at 8:00 A.M. on October 15. About this same time, the outer fringes of the storm first touched the U.S. coastline near North Island, South Carolina. Finally, between 9:30 and 10:00 A.M., Hazel's ominous eye swept inland very near the North Carolina–South Carolina border. It was there on the coast that its most awesome forces were unleashed, although the destruction continued as the hurricane barreled across the state.

The storm surge that Hazel delivered to the southern beaches was the greatest in North Carolina's recorded history. The flood reached eighteen feet above mean low water at Calabash. Hazel's surge was made worse by a matter of pure coincidence — it had struck at the exact time of the highest lunar tide of the year — the full moon of October. Local hunters often refer to this as the

"marsh hen tide," a time when high waters tend to flush waterfowl out of the protective cover of the marsh grass. Hazel's storm tide may have been boosted several feet by the unfortunate timing of its approach.

The coastal region where Hazel made landfall was also battered by some of the most destructive winds in North Carolina's history. Estimates of 150-mph extremes were reported from several locations, including Holden Beach, Calabash, and Little River Inlet. Winds of 98 mph were measured in Wilmington and were estimated at 125 mph at Wrightsville Beach and 140 mph at Oak Island. As Hazel swept inland, its winds endured with freakish intensity. Grannis Airport in Fayetteville reported gusts of 110 mph, and estimates of 120 mph were made by observers in Goldsboro, Kinston, and Faison. At the Raleigh-Durham Airport, the wind-speed dial was watched closely during the storm, and gusts to 90 mph were recorded around 1:30 P.M. Most incredibly, wind gusts near 100 mph were reported from numerous locations in Virginia, Maryland, Pennsylvania, Delaware, New Jersey, and New York as Hazel curved a path through the Northeast on its way to Canada.

Hazel's violent winds hacked or toppled countless trees across eastern North Carolina. In the aftermath of the storm, some sections of highway were littered with "hundreds of trees per mile." Some were uprooted and tossed about, and others were snapped off ten to twenty feet above the ground. In the city of Raleigh, it was reported that an average of two or three trees per block fell. Many fell on cars, homes, and other structures, and power lines were left tangled and broken. Dozens of other cities and towns in the eastern half of the state faced similar losses.

Effects of the hurricane as it moved inland were remarkable. According to a report from the National Weather Service,

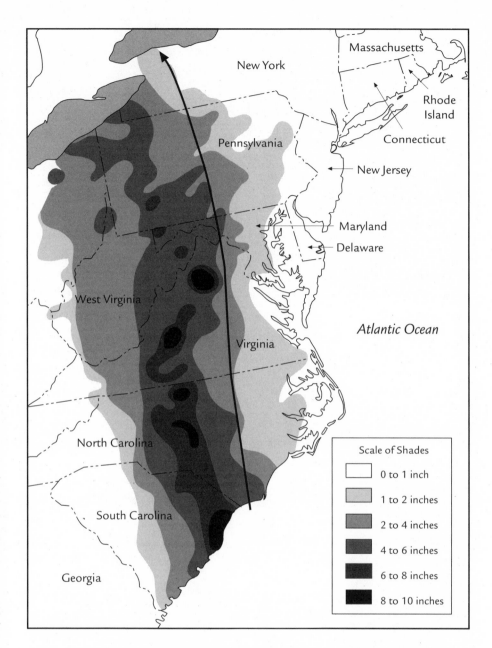

Massachusetts

New York

Rhode Island

Connecticut

Pennsylvania

New Jersey

Maryland

Delaware

West Virginia

Virginia

Atlantic Ocean

North Carolina

South Carolina

Georgia

Scale of Shades

	0 to 1 inch
	1 to 2 inches
	2 to 4 inches
	4 to 6 inches
	6 to 8 inches
	8 to 10 inches

Forests of pine and other trees appeared to be scorched by fire. All trees and plants along the coast appeared to have been burned. Groves of pecan trees were heavily damaged. Building destruction is said to have been greater in the interior sections of North Carolina than at inland points near the coast. From all indications, the hurricane did not decrease in intensity as it moved into the interior.

Inland, out of reach of the rising waters, a tremendous area of North Carolina received heavy damage from high winds. An estimated one-third of all buildings east of the 80th parallel received some damage. Roofs and television aerials were the most widely hit but some radio towers, outdoor theaters, and many signboards were counted among the losses.

Heavy rains fell from northeastern South Carolina to central North Carolina and Virginia. The areas that recorded the greatest rainfall amounts were all on the western side of the storm track, and many eastern locations received as little as one inch. At least ten stations in North Carolina established new twenty-four-hour records for rainfall. These records included about 6.5 inches for Burlington, High Point, and Lexington and 9.72 inches in Carthage, located in the sandhills area of the state. A U.S. Geological Survey rain gauge at Robbins, several miles north of Carthage, measured 11.25 inches. Several locations in northern Virginia recorded more than 10 inches, and new rainfall records were established all along Hazel's northern course.

Although Hazel's most awesome destruction occurred in eastern North Carolina, its inland track through the mid-Atlantic and northern states was unexpectedly intense. After passing Goldsboro and Raleigh at about 1:30 P.M. on October 15, the storm passed through Warren County and into Virginia at about 2:30 that afternoon. At that time, the storm's barometric pressure had only risen to 28.50 inches, up less than one inch from its recorded low near Cape Fear of 27.70.

Hazel accelerated significantly as it passed through Virginia, attaining a forward speed of almost 50 mph. Within four hours, the hurricane had passed over the state, dumping torrential rains and unleashing winds gusting to 100 mph. The storm center passed just west of Richmond, yet winds there were some 30 mph less than in Norfolk, which was on the eastern edge of the storm.

Damages in Virginia were extensive from both winds and tides. Several ships in the James River were either sunk or wrecked, including the battleship *Kentucky*, which broke its moorings and ran aground some one thousand feet from its berth. In all, thirteen Virginians were killed during Hazel, and damages for the state were conservatively estimated at $15 million.

Power failures were commonplace as the storm churned its way through Maryland, the District of Columbia, and Pennsylvania. Wind gusts of 98 mph were reported in Washington, D.C., at 5:07 P.M., and strong winds brought down trees, power lines, and radio towers throughout the region. Winds in Baltimore reached 84 mph, and a six-foot tide flooded streets and basements near Baltimore harbor. Wilmington, Delaware, reported gusts to 98 mph, and Philadelphia recorded gusts to 94 mph. Property damages mounted as Hazel sped relentlessly to the north.

As heavy rains poured out across western Pennsylvania, flash floods swept away cars and homes, and twenty-six lives were lost. The death toll throughout Hazel's northern course was already high, as twenty-two had perished in Virginia, Maryland, Delaware, and the District of Columbia. Then, as the storm raced through western New York state, more tragedies occurred. There, twenty-one deaths were attributed to the hurricane, of which five were caused by falling objects, five by electric shock, four by automobile accidents, three by falls, and four by other causes.

Very few hurricanes in recorded history have maintained their vigor the way Hazel did as it blasted through the interior sections of the northeastern states. As the storm passed through the western counties of New York, winds near 100 mph continued to uproot trees, peel back roofs, and snarl power lines. Then, at approximately 10:00 P.M., just twelve hours after the hurricane had made landfall on the Carolina coast, Hazel joined forces with a weak low-pressure system near Buffalo. Extremely heavy rain fell on numerous communities in western New York, and some city streets were flooded by almost two feet of water. Many highways and bridges were washed out, and the effects of wind and water once again intensified.

As Hazel crossed Lake Ontario, it carried its rampage into Canada. Several locations reported wind gusts of 110 mph. More than seven inches of rain turned the Humber River, which flows along the western edge of Toronto, into a torrent, washing away homes and automobiles. Scores of victims were trapped in the flash flood that swept through the Toronto area. Here, the tragedies continued, as seventy-eight more lives were lost and property damages were estimated at $100 million.

Hazel was last seen crossing the Arctic Circle on its way to Scandinavia, where it eventually fell apart. This incredible hurricane had not lost its momentum and faded away as many storms do when they move over land. Instead, Hazel's destruction was spread over two thousand miles on its northward trek from the Caribbean through North America.

In North Carolina, the destruction left by Hazel was likened to the battlefields of Europe after World War II. Evidence of the storm's violent winds stretched across the state, leaving residents with the task of cleaning up virtually every city street and country road in the eastern half of the state. And the storm tide that swept over the Brunswick and New Hanover beaches brought massive destruction to the coast and was, by all accounts, unparalleled in Tar Heel history.

When Hazel made landfall at Little River, near the North Carolina–South Carolina state line, its deadly storm surge and intense winds reached their peak. At Myrtle Beach, hurricane-force winds began around 6:00 A.M. and continued to intensify until the eye reached the coast at 9:20 A.M. The South Carolina beaches were battered by northeast winds estimated at 130 mph and waves that crested at thirty feet. Hardest hit were locations near the point of landfall, which included Garden City, North Myrtle, Windy Hill, Cherry Grove,

Wreckage filled the waterfront streets of Southport after hurricane Hazel. (Photo by Art Newton; courtesy of the State Port Pilot*)*

Debris was piled high around the amusement center at Ocean Isle. The Brunswick County beaches suffered the most extensive damages from Hazel. (Photo courtesy of the Cape Fear Museum)

and Ocean Drive. Throughout this stretch of coastline, storm-surge levels ranged between fourteen and seventeen feet above mean low water. Although the destruction in South Carolina was greatest on the northern beaches, homes and piers were damaged as far south as Georgetown. Hazel killed one person in South Carolina and brought $27 million in property damages to the state.

Across the border in North Carolina, the south-facing beaches of Brunswick County caught the brunt of Hazel's fury. Robinson Beach, Ocean Isle, Holden Beach, and Long Beach were hardest hit; virtually every home or structure was washed away or severely damaged. In most cases, oceanfront

The National Guard was posted along the beachfront following hurricane Hazel to guard against looting and to restrict sightseers. (Photo courtesy of the Cape Fear Museum)

At Long Beach, most of the cottages that once lined the strand were destroyed by Hazel's seventeen-foot storm surge. Many were washed over into marsh thickets on the leeward side of the island. In the weeks following the storm, some owners hired crews to salvage their cottages by pulling them out of the marsh and repositioning them on the beach. (Photo courtesy of Hugh Morton)

cottages were first battered by waves and 150-mph winds, then swept off their foundations and tossed several hundred yards into marsh thickets. Those unlucky souls who were caught in Hazel's rapidly rising storm tide either rode out the upheaval of their homes or perished in the ordeal.

After surveying the Brunswick beaches in the aftermath of Hazel, the Weather Bureau office in Raleigh issued the following report:

All traces of civilization on that portion of the immediate waterfront between the state line and Cape Fear were practically annihilated. Grass-covered dunes some 10 to 20 feet high along and behind which beach homes had been built in a continuous line 5 miles long simply disappeared, dunes, houses, and all. The paved roadway along which the houses were built was partially washed away, partially buried beneath several feet of sand. The greater part of the material from which the houses had been built was washed from one to two hundred yards back into the edge of low-lying woods which cover the leeward side of the islands. Some of this material is identifiable as having been parts of houses, but the greater portion of it is ground to unrecognizable splinters and bits of masonry. Of the 357 buildings which existed on Long Beach, 352 were totally destroyed and the other five damaged. Similar conditions prevail on Holden Beach, Ocean Isle, Robinson Beach, and Colonial Beach. In most cases it is impossible to tell where the buildings stood. Where grassy dunes once stood there is now only flat, white, sandy beach.

The *State Port Pilot* reported the story of two survivors who endured the worst of the storm: Connie and Jerry Helms. The couple had come to Long Beach for their honeymoon and were out roller-skating the night before Hazel struck. The Coast Guard warned other residents of the hurricane's approach, but the newlyweds arrived back at the beach too late to hear the warnings. They went to bed with no knowledge of the ominous storm poised off the coast.

At dawn the next morning, the Helmses awoke to the sound of pounding surf and chairs blowing about their porch. Huge waves began crashing over the dunes as the couple scrambled to leave their cottage. With no time to even pack their clothes, they jumped into their car, but it wouldn't start. They ran to their jeep, but it wouldn't start either. By this time, the surging ocean water was waist deep in the street, and they knew it was becoming deeper and rougher by the minute. They made their way to a nearby two-story house and broke through a door to get inside. As the tides continued to rise, the second floor buckled and the couple feared they might perish if the house collapsed.

"We started seeing houses exploding then floating away," Jerry Helms recalled. "Sometimes you could see the whole house flying through the air. There was a little cinderblock house next door, and a breaker went over top of the house, and after it went over it was gone. Stoves, refrigerators, and houses were flying through the air. Before we got out of the house we were in, we saw a guy standing in the doorway of another house floating by. He was found the next day buried in the sand."

The couple watched as the entire island went underwater and every house within sight was swept away or pounded to splinters by massive waves. Large timbers, roof sections, and appliances of every kind whisked past the cottage where they had taken refuge. Then, as the water swirled just inches below the second-story windows, the Helmses knew that their shelter was about to give in to the storm's waves and winds. Tying themselves together with a flannel blanket, the newlyweds escaped the collapsing house through a high window. Connie Helms, who could not swim, climbed onto a cotton mattress while her husband jumped into the raging waters.

"We went right out to sea on that mattress," Jerry recalled. "By that time, all the two-story houses were covered by water, and most of the other stuff was already gone. But we never had a chance to think about what was happening or be scared. We were just trying to hold on to that blanket and stay alive."

The currents did not take the couple out to sea but instead carried them toward the leeward side of the island. To stabilize their makeshift life raft, Jerry grabbed a section of a house that drifted by and positioned their mattress on top of it. A short time later, their raft became lodged in some treetops near Davis Creek. There the couple endured the storm for several more hours.

"It got real calm when the eye passed over, and then it started raining real hard. It felt like little bullets," Jerry recalled. "There was a lot of times we thought we were gone. The only thing that saved us was the good Lord and that blanket."

When the hurricane winds subsided and the floodwaters receded, the Helmses climbed down from the treetops. They then made their way across Davis Canal — still clutching the blanket that had helped save their lives. The couple later found their way to Southport, where they visited Dosher Memorial Hospital for treatment. Later that night they went back to their home in Whiteville.

The following day, Jerry Helms returned to Long Beach to search for the remains of the car, the jeep, and the cottage. Both vehicles were buried deep in the sand, and the only remaining fragment of the house was one corner, held in place by a single post. About a mile up the beach, he found his refrigerator, still intact, with its door sealed. "The drinks in the refrigerator were still cold and the only thing broken was a bowl of peas, so we sat down and ate lunch out of it," he said. The honeymoon was over for the Helmses, but their incredible struggle for survival was not soon forgotten.

Several miles west of Long Beach, the resort of Ocean Isle was the scene of the single greatest tragedy Hazel brought to the Carolinas. The beach was connected to the mainland by a small ferry that was destroyed in the early stages of the storm. Given no means of escape, a group of eleven people gathered in one of the island's larger buildings to rise above the oncoming storm surge. As the winds and waves increased, the building began to crumble, forcing the group to swim through the breakers to a nearby truck. With the women and children inside, the men tried in vain to keep the vehicle upright as the tides continued to rise. Tragically, their efforts were no match for Hazel's fury and the truck was soon washed away. Of the eleven, only two survived. Thirty-three cottages that had stood on Ocean Isle were completely de-

stroyed. Only two houses remained, and they were washed almost one mile across the island into the marsh.

In Southport, Hazel's storm tide forced ocean water through the mouth of the Cape Fear River, flooding the waterfront streets with a surge of eight feet. All twenty of the town's shrimp houses and fuel docks were destroyed. Restaurants along the river and several warehouses were demolished. The storm tide lifted thirty-five-ton shrimp trawlers over the seawall and swept them into town, crushing cars and homes along the way. Along Bay Street, majestic old oak trees were toppled by winds near 140 mph. For several blocks near the waterfront, large piles of debris choked the town's streets.

As hurricane Hazel came ashore on the morning of October 15, 1954, the people of Southport scrambled to avoid the storm's rapidly rising tide. The surge wrecked the many shrimp houses that lined the riverfront and carried the remaining debris far into the town's streets. (Photo by Art Newton; courtesy of the State Port Pilot)

The Southport waterfront after Hazel. (Photo by Art Newton; courtesy of the State Port Pilot*)*

Lewis Hardee owned two trawlers and a shrimp-packing house on the Southport waterfront. As the storm reached its peak, his boats floated over the docks and his shrimp house was destroyed. Like many others in the small town, Hardee made his living on the water. "Back then, nobody had insurance on boats in Southport," Hardee recalled. "Things were a mess. Boats were scattered all in the marsh from the Intercoastal [waterway] to the Coast Guard Station. We all had a warning, but nobody knew it would be like it was."

Hardee had just rebuilt his shrimp house and dock the summer before

Portions of Caswell Beach were swept clean by Hazel's storm tide, which broke apart the only road down the beach. (Photo courtesy of Mrs. J. T. Barnes)

Southport after hurricane Hazel. (Photo by Art Newton; courtesy of the State Port Pilot*)*

Hazel arrived and tore them apart. A fire the previous year had damaged the old structures, and his new pier and house had been built with costly cypress. Hazel's powerful winds and waves broke them to pieces and scattered their timbers along the shore. "After the storm, I took a carpenter's crayon and went along the waterfront and put my name on every board," Hardee remembers. "You know they weren't hardly seasoned, they were new lumber, just a year old. All two-inch cypress decking. With that lumber I built another new fish house down at the yacht basin."

After Hazel passed, the fishermen of Southport faced the challenge of removing their large trawlers from high ground, repairing their damaged hulls, and returning them to the water. Fortunately, a contractor at the nearby ammunition facility at Sunny Point offered assistance in this effort. A crew from Diamond Construction Company brought in an eighty-five-foot crane that lifted the large boats from the streets and yards of Southport and placed them back in the water. This task took several days, but the residents and fishermen of this storm-ravaged town were grateful for the help.

Farther up the river in Wilmington, flooding in the Cape Fear reached its highest level in recorded history. Floodwaters damaged numerous warehouses along the waterfront, and dozens of cars were submerged by the rising water. Overall damage to the city was not extensive and was limited mostly to broken storefront windows and uprooted trees. High winds snapped telephone poles in several locations, leaving more than half the area's residents without any means of communication. Wilmington was without electricity for three days. Two thousand residents were sheltered in twenty Red Cross evacuation centers around the city.

Diamond Construction Company came to the aid of Southport residents by delivering a large crane to remove wayward boats from the town's streets. (Photo courtesy of Leila H. Pigott)

The Wilmington Reserve fleet in the Brunswick River basin suffered about $1 million in damage from the storm. Several of the large ships broke their mooring lines when high winds "snapped cable an inch and five-eights in diameter like it was ribbon." Three liberty ships drifted upriver with the winds and threatened to wreck the Brunswick River bridge. At the peak of the storm, a tugboat captain made a heroic effort to stop the ships just one hundred yards from the bridge. His courageous efforts saved the concrete span that provided the only link between Brunswick and New Hanover Counties.

Carolina Beach was hit hard by Hazel, largely because the popular resort found itself in the hurricane's powerful northeast section. Property damage

there totaled $17 million, much more than in any other coastal community. The heaviest damages occurred along the oceanfront, where the storm's tidal surge bashed homes and the downtown amusement area. In all, 362 buildings were completely destroyed and another 288 suffered major damage.

A number of residents stayed on Carolina Beach through the hurricane and witnessed Hazel's attack on their town. They saw large waves roll through Mack's 5 & 10 store and watched as the steel pier collapsed and sank. Dozens of houses floated off their foundations and "crashed together like bumper cars." One man was crouched in his living room when a surging wave heaved an eight-by-eight-inch timber through four walls of his home. After the hurricane passed, the giant piece of lumber had to be cut into four pieces to be removed.

According to a story by Susan Gerdes that appeared in the *Tidewater*, eighty-year-old Alex McEachern refused to leave his Carolina Beach home upon Hazel's approach. To escape the rising waters, he and his dog climbed atop a freezer in his pantry to ride out the storm. Miraculously, even though Mc-

Deep sand filled the streets of Carolina Beach after hurricane Hazel. National Guard troops patrolled the area to search for storm victims and to protect homes and businesses from looting. (Photo courtesy of the Cape Fear Museum)

Alice Strickland, town clerk of Carolina Beach, remained in the small town hall during hurricane Hazel. Undaunted, she cheerfully directs workers while the receding storm tide swirls around her knees. (From Making a Difference in North Carolina, *by Ed Rankin and Hugh Morton; photo courtesy of Hugh Morton)*

Eachern's house was torn apart by the wind and waves, the pantry was unharmed; in fact it was the only room left standing. After the storm subsided, the lucky twosome climbed down from their refuge and found their way into town.

During the early part of the storm, emergency workers used the Carolina Beach Town Hall auditorium as disaster headquarters. But as the floodwaters rose, town officials packed up their equipment and important documents and retreated to the China Cafe, which stood on slightly higher ground. Ultimately, fourteen blocks of the town were underwater. One house caught fire

The Breakers Hotel, Wilmington Beach. (Photo courtesy of the Cape Fear Museum)

A sentry stands guard in downtown Carolina Beach. There were reports in the days following Hazel that looters were launching boats and even swimming over to the storm-ravaged resort communities of Carolina and Wrightsville Beaches. (Photo courtesy of the Cape Fear Museum)

Carolina Beach during hurricane Hazel. (Photo courtesy of Hugh Morton)

during the storm, but firefighters were unable to reach it because of the flood. As officials looked on, the residence burned down to the waterline, which was about four feet above the ground.

Up the coast at Wrightsville Beach, Hazel's storm surge ruined dozens of large oceanfront cottages. Estimated at twelve feet above mean low water, the

The first row of cottages facing the ocean at Wrightsville Beach was eliminated by Hazel's storm surge. (Photo courtesy of Hugh Morton)

tide swept over the island, destroying 89 buildings and severely damaging another 155. Property damages were estimated at $7 million, including severe destruction to the town's sewage plant.

When Hazel struck the Wilmington area, only twelve state troopers were on duty, but additional support was brought in quickly. By the following day, fifty troopers from as far away as Asheville had come to assist local police with the around-the-clock task of maintaining checkpoints, directing traffic, and assisting those in need. Numerous accounts of heroic rescues were compiled after the storm, including several rescues made on foot in chest-deep water. Many local officers were said to have faithfully maintained their duties while their own homes were demolished in the storm.

Checkpoints were set up in key locations to prevent immediate access to the hard-hit barrier islands. Thousands of eager sightseers traveled to the coast to witness the destruction, but most were turned away. Looting was a severe

Wrightsville Beach after hurricane Hazel. (Photo courtesy of Hugh Morton)

Wrightsville Beach. (Photo courtesy of the Lower Cape Fear Historical Society)

problem, and on some beaches the National Guard was brought in to assist the police with protecting property. According to local news reports, some looters launched small boats and even swam across the waterways to evade police and made off with radios, stoves, refrigerators, and cash.

Even along the coastline north of Wrightsville there was considerable destruction. At New Topsail Beach, 210 of the 230 houses were destroyed and property damages were estimated at $2.5 million. The Topsail Island drawbridge was "carried away" by Hazel's furious winds and tides, and a Marine Corps amphibious vehicle was the only means of transport to the island for days. Snead's Ferry and Swansboro suffered from extreme high tides, which

Up the coast at Topsail Island, Hazel's storm surge was deadly to the cottages that lined the beach. (Photo courtesy of the Cape Fear Museum)

Hurricane Hazel washed out numerous bridges throughout eastern North Carolina, including this one at Snead's Ferry. (Photo courtesy of the Cape Fear Museum)

deposited fishing boats and pleasure craft high and dry in streets and backyards.

In Carteret County, 120 miles north of where Hazel made landfall, residents witnessed the worst hurricane in many years. Hundreds of citizens took refuge in Morehead City Town Hall and the county courthouse in Beaufort. Damage was extensive in several locations near the water, including Atlantic Beach and the causeway that joins Morehead City and Beaufort. Property damages were reported at $2 million, but fortunately there were no reports of deaths or serious injuries. Thirty-five homes were destroyed, and scores more suffered minor damage.

Even though Hazel's eye passed nearly a hundred miles to the west, Carteret County was within reach of the storm's violent right-front quadrant. High tides flooded parts of Morehead City, as seen in this photo, which was taken looking westward from the old Atlantic Beach bridge. (Photo courtesy Clifton Guthrie)

In Atlantic Beach, Hazel's storm surge pounded the boardwalk area to rubble. Twenty-foot waves washed away a section of the Atlantic Beach Hotel. On the other end of the boardwalk, waves washed through the lobby of the Ocean King Hotel, undermining the structure. The Triple S fishing pier was battered by the surf and its tackle shop was badly damaged. After the storm, only two hundred of the pier's one thousand feet remained. The old beach highway that connected Salter Path and Emerald Isle was swept away in two places. In these areas, Bogue Sound connected with the ocean, but only briefly, until heavy equipment was brought in to fill in the overwash.

In Morehead City, a fish house, dwelling, and skating rink were washed from their foundations. Large glass windows were smashed and trees were

An eight-foot storm surge battered the Pavilion at Atlantic Beach. (Photo courtesy of the Carteret County News-Times)

Front Street in Beaufort was under several feet of water during hurricane Hazel. At the peak of the storm, water nearly covered the parking meters shown here. (Photo courtesy of the Carteret County News-Times)

toppled by winds that gusted to near 100 mph. At the peak of the storm, surging waters flooded the basement of the Morehead City hospital. For hours, fire trucks pumped the water out so that basement facilities could continue to be used. Nurses in the basement worked with water up to their knees, scrambling to remove patients and save equipment.

Tony Seamon of Morehead City witnessed the effect Hazel had on the county. He and his father ventured downtown during the storm. "Daddy wanted to check on the restaurant," Seamon recalled. "We drove down Twentieth Street and the wind whipped the water across the road. We came to the

Oceanfront destruction in Atlantic Beach after Hazel.

old wooden picket bridge and it was submerged. The only way we could drive through that water was to open both car doors and let the water come on through."

As they reached downtown Morehead, Seamon's dad asked him to investigate the damage to the restaurant. "He told me, 'You got to get out and look inside,'" Seamon remembered. After one failed attempt to wade through the waist-deep water, he tried again to make it to the Sanitary Restaurant. "The current through the street was like a river. I eventually went under swimming to avoid the wind. When I got to the restaurant, I could look through the door and see all the tables and chairs floating around. Daddy had made the decision to cut holes in the floor to equalize the pressure. At least the whole place didn't float away."

After the hurricane passed, the Sanitary Restaurant was cleaned up and put into service as a feeding center. The Red Cross set up generators to provide power, food was brought in, and coupons were issued for meals. Work crews involved in cleanup efforts were fed around the clock until power was restored to the area and things returned to "normal."

Other portions of Carteret County were hit hard by the storm. Several homes along the Morehead-Beaufort Causeway were totally wrecked, and their debris was piled high in the middle of Highway 70. Huge waves rolled across the causeway for hours, washing away homes and depositing small skiffs and one large cruiser in the roadway. Several cars were abandoned by their owners on the east side of the Beaufort bridge when the unwary motorists became trapped by the hurricane's surging tide. The cars choked when

water completely covered their engines, and the drivers were forced to wade through the tide to safety.

In Beaufort, the downtown businesses along Front Street suffered heavy losses. Every store was flooded with seawater, which covered the entire street to a depth of three feet. Gusting winds caused plate-glass windows in numerous stores to shatter, resulting in even greater damage from wind-driven rain. City Appliance Company, Bell's Drug Store, and Merrill's Men's Store were among the hardest hit. Numerous small boats were washed into the streets, and at least four cabin cruisers sank in Taylor's Creek. The highest water in Beaufort occurred at 11:15 A.M., when the barometer fell to its low point (for

Hurricane Connie damaged numerous cottages in Atlantic Beach, many of which had only recently been repaired following hurricane Hazel the previous year. (Photo courtesy of Robert Lewis)

Carteret County) of 29.06 inches. The tides in Morehead reached their peak an hour later, around noon.

Across the county, Hazel battered homes, boats, and utilities. Many houses that had just been reshingled after hurricane Edna were stripped again by gusts of 90 to 100 mph. Power lines and poles were tangled and communications were cut. A section of the North River Bridge was washed away, but rapid work by state highway crews had the bridge repaired just five days after the storm.

Although the Pamlico and Albemarle Sounds region was on the eastern edge of Hazel's course through the state, numerous communities throughout the area suffered serious flooding. The Outer Banks north of Ocracoke were not severely affected, but cities such as Washington and Belhaven saw extensive damage from the rising tides. New Bern, Edenton, and Elizabeth City also reported flooding. But across a wide portion of inland North Carolina, far from the effects of the tides, Hazel's powerful winds brought significant destruction to more than two dozen counties.

Although most of Hazel's fatalities in North Carolina occurred along the beaches of Brunswick County, several deaths resulted from the harrowing winds that raced across the state. In Wallace, a tobacco warehouse collapsed, crushing a Warsaw man underneath the rubble. In Parkton, a one-month-old infant was killed when a large tree fell through her home. The child's mother

Hurricane Connie was followed so closely by hurricane Diane that the floods affecting much of eastern North Carolina had little time to subside. Sounds and rivers like the Pamlico spread far beyond their banks. (Photo courtesy of Roy Hardee)

was seriously injured, as she had been lying next to her daughter in bed when the massive tree came crashing down. Other deaths occurred as a result of electrocution, falls, and automobile accidents. Across North Carolina, hospital emergency rooms were filled with victims of the storm. At least two hundred injuries were reported, some serious, in the six hours Hazel visited the state.

By most accounts, it was the most destructive hurricane in Tar Heel history. In North Carolina the toll was heavy: nineteen people killed and over two hundred injured; fifteen thousand homes and structures destroyed; thirty-nine thousand structures damaged; thirty counties with major damage; and an estimated $136 million in property losses. But when the hurricane's effects in North Carolina are combined with those of the other states, as well as with those of Canada and Haiti, the numbers climb: over six hundred dead and an estimated $350 million in property damage. And of course, the damages are in 1954 dollars.

The great hurricane of October 1954 became a benchmark in the lives of many North Carolinians who endured the storm. From Holden Beach to Henderson and everywhere in between, anytime the topic of hurricanes is raised, stories about Hazel are sure to follow. Stories of heroic rescues and tragic losses are well remembered, as are testimonials to the awesome destructive forces

Shop owners in Washington, N.C., piled sandbags at their doors to try to keep Diane's floodwaters from pouring inside their businesses. (Photo courtesy of Roy Hardee)

the storm displayed. Hazel ranks as one of the most catastrophic hurricanes to strike the United States in the twentieth century. Fortunately, storms of its magnitude are relatively rare events, and few other hurricanes deserve comparison with it. But much to the dismay of the people of eastern North Carolina, the active 1954 hurricane season that had spawned Carol, Edna, and Hazel was merely a prelude to the 1955 season, when three more storms would strike the state.

CONNIE (AUGUST 12, 1955)

Less than one year after Hazel carved its way through the Carolinas, residents along the Tar Heel coast braced themselves for the approach of another serious storm—hurricane Connie. As it turned out, however, Connie was only the first of three hurricanes to make landfall in North Carolina during the 1955 season. Hurricane Diane followed closely on Connie's heels, and hurricane Ione arrived a month later. All three storms spun across the state in one frightening six-week period, between August 12 and September 20. These three events brought unprecedented destruction to the eastern counties and compounded the earlier damages caused by Hazel.

As hurricane Connie passed north of Puerto Rico on August 6, reconnaissance crews measured its barometric pressure at 27.88 inches and estimated its maximum winds to be near 145 mph. By August 8, Connie's forward movement had slowed considerably, and the storm wobbled erratically as it approached the Carolinas. By the time it crossed over Cape Lookout on the morning of August 12, Connie's intensity had decreased considerably. After

passing through the Pamlico and Albemarle Sounds region, it continued northward up Chesapeake Bay before turning to the northwest. On August 14, Connie dissipated somewhere over Lake Huron.

As Connie moved across the North Carolina coastline its winds were barely of hurricane force. Wilmington reported sustained winds of 72 mph with gusts of 83 mph. Winds of 75 mph were reported at Fort Macon, with gusts that reached 100 mph. Wind damages were relatively light along the coast, although some television aerials and roof shingles that had been repaired after Hazel were lost.

Before Connie moved ashore in Carteret County, and while it was still staggering about in the Atlantic, several tornadoes were reported in the Carolinas. Early in the evening on August 10, five twisters touched down in South Carolina, from Georgetown northward. One was reported near Penderlea, North Carolina, where five buildings were demolished and one person was injured. These tornadoes were most likely spawned in the broad spiral rainbands that extended from the center of hurricane Connie.

Although overall wind destruction from Connie was light, torrential rains and prolonged high tides brought extensive flooding to the North Carolina coast. For several days the storm moved sluggishly, and broad-scale winds over the Atlantic pushed a high mound of water toward the shore. Connie's slow movement across the state aggravated the situation as tremendous rains were dumped on the eastern counties. The result was that thousands of acres of farmland were flooded by a combination of extreme high tides and heavy runoff.

Huge waves pounded the coastline, and beach erosion was said to have been

Hurricane Diane made landfall just five days after hurricane Connie in August 1955. Although Diane was a category-one storm when it hit, it went on to become one of our nation's most tragic hurricanes. (Photo courtesy of the News and Observer Publishing Co./N.C. Division of Archives and History)

The National Guard was available in Belhaven to evacuate residents in need during hurricane Diane. (Photo courtesy of Roy Hardee)

worse than that caused by Hazel. Tides were about seven feet above normal on the beaches from Southport to Nags Head, and flooding in the sounds and near the mouths of rivers was estimated to range from five to eight feet.

At Morehead City, near where Connie's irregular eye crossed the coastline, almost 12 inches of rain were recorded. Heavy rains fell throughout the mid-Atlantic states as the storm dragged slowly northward. Amounts in excess of 9 inches were measured in eastern Pennsylvania, New Jersey, and Delaware. At La Guardia Field in New York, 12.20 inches of rain were recorded in a thirty-eight-hour period on August 12–13.

DIANE (AUGUST 17, 1955)

Although the heavy rains from Connie did not bring extensive damages to North Carolina or the Northeast, they did saturate the ground, overfill rivers and streams, and set the stage for the record-breaking floods of hurricane Diane. Diane followed so closely behind Connie that coastal residents had little time to prepare for its approach. And no one was prepared for the deadly flash floods that swept through the Northeast.

Because the two hurricanes hit just days apart, officials were unable to as-

sess the damages from each separately, and many records were combined. Connie and Diane delivered a one-two punch to a broad region, as floods from Diane were amplified by the soaked soils from the previous storm. Diane's heavy rains brought flash floods to several states. These floods killed two hundred and established a new record in destruction—Diane was declared by some to be the first "billion-dollar hurricane."

The very day Connie raked over the North Carolina coastline, Diane reached hurricane intensity some one thousand miles at sea. For a while, Diane turned toward the open ocean, possibly influenced by the movements of Connie. But then the storm veered to the northwest and curved toward the North Carolina coast. In the early morning hours of August 17, just five days after Connie's arrival, hurricane Diane moved inland over Carolina Beach.

Ship reports had indicated that Diane's winds were near 125 mph while it was at sea. But fortunately, and as with Connie, its intensity dropped as it approached land. Winds of 50 mph were reported at Cape Hatteras, and a gust of 74 mph was recorded in Wilmington. These gusts had a minimal effect on the coastal region, and wind-damage reports were primarily from inland counties that suffered crop damage.

But as with Connie, Diane's wind-driven tides and torrential rains brought extensive flooding to the Tar Heel coast. Tides associated with Diane were generally higher than those of the previous hurricane and ranged from five to nine feet above mean low water along the beaches. Some coastal rivers and sounds also crested at nine feet above normal. In Belhaven, the water rose three feet above floor level in the business district. In some portions of downtown New Bern and Washington water was "waist deep." Flooding in the Cape Fear River was extreme, and damages were reported along the Wilmington city docks. In all, one thousand people were evacuated from the low-lying areas and towns near the water's edge.

In Carteret County, Diane had similar effects. Residents were still reeling from Connie when the warnings were issued that a second storm was approaching. Some shop owners in Beaufort lined their doors with sandbags in hopes that rising waters might be kept at bay. High tides brought flooding to most causeways and bridges, and the North River Bridge was once again put "out" by the storm. The motor on the Atlantic Beach drawbridge burned out just prior to Diane's arrival, and prisoners from nearby Newport Prison were brought in to turn the steel span by hand. Twenty-three homes at Salter Path were damaged by high water, but artificial sand dunes hastily built after Connie helped limit the destruction to many beachfront homes.

But along many southern beaches and as far north as Cape Hatteras, beach erosion was severe. Diane's slow movement to the northwest caused prolonged winds to push salt water out of Pamlico Sound and into the farms and fields of the east. Thousands of acres were flooded again, just as they had been during Connie. Supplementing this tidal flood, Diane dumped heavy rains across the state. But although North Carolina was inundated by the combined effects of the two August hurricanes, the flooding and rainfall that followed in the Northeast delivered the catastrophic destruction for which Diane is remembered.

After it came ashore on the beaches of New Hanover County, Diane continued on a steady inland track. By midafternoon on August 17, the storm center had passed over the Raleigh-Durham Airport and was beginning to curve gently into Virginia. By the early morning hours of the eighteenth, it had begun to turn toward the northeast, and it passed near Lynchburg, Virginia, on its way through Philadelphia, Atlantic City, and Nantucket, Massachusetts. While the storm tracked northward through Virginia, winds diminished to only 35 mph. Diane's winds were of little consequence when compared with the record-breaking rains that were unleashed as the hurricane drifted to the northeast. Several locations along the eastern slopes of the Blue Ridge Mountains received in excess of ten inches, and portions of eastern New York and southern New England recorded over twelve inches within a twenty-four-hour period. A report from the National Weather Service detailed some of the destruction: "The excessive rains of hurricane Diane fell on many of the same localities previously drenched by rains associated with hurricane Connie, and

Governor Luther H. Hodges examines a tracking chart to study the path of the next approaching hurricane, Ione, in September 1955. (Photo courtesy of the News and Observer Publishing Co./ N.C. Division of Archives and History)

combined they produced the most devastating floods the valleys of eastern Pennsylvania, northwestern New Jersey, southeastern New York and southern New England have ever experienced. In the vicinity of Stroudsburg, Pa., 75 persons lost their lives when rapidly rising water from Broadhead Creek swept away a summer camp. The floods in Virginia and portions of North Carolina and West Virginia were damaging in some localities, but less severe than those in the northeastern states."

By late in the afternoon on August 19, Diane was on its way back to sea, where it died quietly over the North Atlantic. It is estimated that the storm claimed close to two hundred lives during its two-day visit, and almost all were lost in the deadly flash floods that washed through the Northeast. Initial damage estimates exceeded $800 million, surpassing all other hurricanes in U.S. history. Ironically, the vast majority of the destruction occurred not along the coastline but in the inland sections of several states.

In North Carolina, no lives were lost during either Connie or Diane, but damages from the two storms exceeded $80 million. Twenty-two counties were affected by the hurricanes' winds and water, and numerous construction projects still under repair from previous storms were undermined. Connie had registered as a category-three hurricane when it hit, Diane as a category two. Neither storm matched Hazel in intensity or local destruction, but many

North Carolinians were beginning to wonder what wrath had fallen upon them. In churches across the state, special "hurricane prayer" services were held to comfort victims and build hope for more peaceful times.

IONE (SEPTEMBER 19, 1955)

The 1955 hurricane season in North Carolina did not end with Connie and Diane. One month after Diane's departure, hurricane Ione struck the coast near Salter Path, a few miles west of Atlantic Beach. Ione became the third significant hurricane to make landfall that summer, something of a rare occurrence in North Carolina. Ione eventually inundated record portions of the coastal plain and established new high-water marks in numerous locations. Several new records for rainfall were also recorded across the state.

Like many September hurricanes, Ione was born out of an easterly wave that passed through the Cape Verde Islands on September 6. By the time it reached the western Atlantic and was in position to threaten the Carolina coast, Ione was a major storm. On September 17, it reached peak intensity with sustained winds of 125 mph and a central pressure of 27.70 inches. When it crossed the coastline at 5:00 A.M. on the nineteenth, the pressure had risen to about 28.00 inches and winds had diminished considerably. Ione's winds gusted at around 100 mph in several locations. The highest winds were measured at Cherry Point, where sustained winds of 75 mph and a gust of 107 mph were recorded. The hurricane continued to weaken as it returned to sea off the Virginia coast.

Incredible amounts of rain were dumped on the eastern counties as Ione dragged its heavy clouds across the region. A report from the National Weather Service described the record flooding:

As Ione crossed the coastline in the vicinity of Morehead City, hurricane associated rains continued for a long period. Most of the damage caused by hurricane Ione was by flooding to crops. According to the State Climatologist at Raleigh, between August 10 and the approach of Ione, eastern North Carolina had been repeatedly drenched with heavy rains with more than 30 inches falling in the wettest sections. The some 16 inches which fell in the same areas with the passage of Ione brought 45-day precipitation totals to values without precedent in the weather history of North Carolina. In the 42-day period August 11 to September 20 the cooperative field station at Maysville reported a rainfall of 48.90 inches. This unprecedented rainfall, approximately one-third of it falling in about 30 hours with hurricane Ione, produced the heaviest runoff of record on downstream tributaries and coastal creeks in North Carolina. The combination of tide waters from the east and flood water from the west inundated the greatest area of eastern

Flooding in New Bern during hurricane Ione. (Photo courtesy of the New Bern–Craven County Public Library)

North Carolina ever known to have flooded. In New Bern, the depth of water which, according to press reports, was 16-feet above normal, was the greatest of record.

In New Bern, the actual flooding was measured at ten and a half feet above mean low water, still one and a half feet greater than the hurricanes of 1913 or 1933. Forty city blocks were flooded; some streets were covered with so much water that parking meters were completely submerged. Many residents were evacuated from their homes by boat. Water measured six feet deep on East Front Street north of Broad Street. By 9:00 A.M. on September 19, the eye of the storm passed just east of New Bern, and the flooding reached its peak. As many as two thousand New Bern residents were sheltered during the storm.

The flooding was so severe across a broad area that rural roads, city streets, and state highways were impassable. Among the highways closed to traffic were N.C. 24, cut by a washout between Swansboro and Morehead City; N.C. 53 near Burgaw; N.C. 172 near Snead's Ferry; U.S. 264 near Washington in Hyde County; N.C. 33, where a bridge was washed out between Aurora and Chocowinity; N.C. 94 across Lake Mattamuskeet; N.C. 11 near Kinston; U.S. 70 near Newport; and U.S. 158, where damages occurred to Little Creek Bridge.

State highway officials reported "anywhere you went, you went in water." Severe damage occurred to the North River Bridge, east of Beaufort. Just as had happened during hurricane Hazel, Ione's tides swept away several wooden spans of the 975-foot drawbridge, immediately isolating three thousand

Carteret County residents. While repairs were being made, amphibious vehicles were brought in to transport supplies and rescue workers to and from the remote down-east areas. In addition, the state highway commission hired a local boat captain to use his trawler for transport.

Man-made sand dunes that had been erected near Atlantic Beach after Diane helped lessen the impact of Ione's storm surge. Mayor Alfred B. Cooper reported that beachfront destruction was not as severe as it had been in the earlier hurricanes. A few houses were undermined and several lost their porches, but overall oceanfront damage was not severe. All of the fishing piers in the Carteret region remained intact after Ione. Near the Morehead–Atlantic Beach Causeway, however, "Mom and Pop's" fishing pier was destroyed by the tide.

The combined effects of Connie, Diane, and Ione were said to have swept away all the dunes along the twenty-five-mile stretch of beach from Cape Lookout to Drum Inlet. This narrow barrier island was "smooth as an airfield" after the storms had passed. Drum Inlet itself was affected by the massive tides and became unnavigable after Ione, when new sand shoals formed and choked the channel. At Sea Level, Otway, Harker's Island, and Beaufort, homes and streets were flooded. Fishing boats and small craft were tossed ashore and wrecked in typical fashion. Along the Beaufort waterfront, numerous businesses were again flooded and store windows were smashed.

The *News and Observer* reported that in Morehead City, the hurricane "raged all day" and was described as the "worst storm in 35 years." More than three feet of water filled many streets. Fish houses, docks, and other structures were washed about, leaving large piles of wrecked lumber along the shore. Winds of 110 mph toppled trees and ripped away shingles and, in some cases, entire roofs. The Morehead City hospital was flooded again during Ione. The basement filled with water just as it had during Hazel, and this time electrical equipment was damaged. Three women were reported to have been in labor during the peak of the storm, but all fared well.

As Ione moved northward through the Pamlico-Albemarle region it slowed and curved to the northeast, passing near Elizabeth City on its way back to the Atlantic. This track carried the hurricane far enough inland to extend damages westward. In Belhaven, most of the town's residents had to be evacuated in amphibious military "ducks." In Aurora, much of the community was inundated and most residents were forced to leave. In Washington, North Carolina, "two-thirds" of the city was flooded as the Pamlico River and numerous creeks overflowed. In Greenville, Ione was described as "more severe and a longer blow than Hazel." In Bethel, Farmville, Plymouth, Elizabeth City, and numerous other down-east communities, damages were severe, especially to crops. Peanuts, tobacco, cotton, and corn were among the hardest hit.

Along the Outer Banks, beach erosion carved away more protective dunes at

Ocracoke and Hatteras Island. Ione had originally been forecast for landfall between Cape Lookout and Cape Hatteras, and residents on Ocracoke were prepared for high waters that never came. Wooden Coca-Cola crates and cinder blocks were used to elevate refrigerators, stoves, freezers, and furniture. One island resident described the preparation in the *News and Observer*:

> People with second storeys are fortunate. Lots of things are laboriously carried upstairs. The loud cackling from a neighbor's yard tells us that the chickens are being caught and being put up on the top roost, with wire stretched beneath it to keep them there. The ducks resent this treatment; they prefer to be penned outside where the swimming is good. The pet dogs and cats are called to safety.
>
> Flashlight batteries, candles, oil, food are stocked for emergency use; also a good supply of drinking water. Two precautions must be observed: 1) before the storm gets too bad and the salt spray begins to blow through the air, disconnect the cistern or water barrel, and 2) before the tide gets too high, let the water come into the house. Don't try to keep it out or you'll float away.

After Ione paid its visit to eastern North Carolina, it turned slowly back to sea, sparing the northeastern states a repeat of the destruction brought on by hurricane Diane. Ione's wobbling, erratic movements were described by officials from the Weather Bureau as "a forecaster's nightmare." Although they had done their best to outguess the storm's next moves, its return to sea was not expected and caused the bureau to issue a false alarm to the northeastern states. Ione did, however, make landfall again in southern Newfoundland, Canada, and was described as "still packing a powerful punch."

Unlike Connie and Diane, Ione was responsible for several deaths in North Carolina. Five persons drowned across the state, including two in New Bern. One of those was a nine-year-old boy who stepped off his front porch into floodwaters that were over his head. Two additional deaths occurred in mishaps involving automobiles. A Camp Lejeune marine was killed when his car crashed through a barricade set up at a washed-out bridge, and a Beaufort man drowned when his car accidently spilled into a roadside canal that was overfilled by floodwaters.

Most of the damages in North Carolina that were directly attributable to Ione resulted from losses to agriculture. Crops were destroyed, topsoil was washed away, and farmland was contaminated by salt water. It was estimated that almost 90,000 acres of land in the eastern part of the state were submerged during the storm. Approximately $46 million in crop damage was reported, while official estimates of Ione's total price tag in North Carolina approached $90 million.

The three storms of 1955 made that year the most expensive in North Caro-

Ione's winds toppled dozens of large trees in downtown New Bern. (Photos courtesy of the New Bern–Craven County Public Library)

lina's hurricane history. Connie, Diane, and Ione together caused $170 million in property and agricultural damage to the state. When combined with the losses from Hazel the previous year, North Carolina faced an economic hardship of unprecedented proportions. Governor Luther H. Hodges testified before the U.S. Senate Appropriations Committee that the four storms had caused a loss of $326 million. That total exceeded the entire state's annual revenue for the year. As an illustration of this great loss, it was noted that "3000 miles of first-class highways might have been built in eastern North Carolina for the money lost to hurricanes." Relief aid was provided by numerous groups and included federal financial assistance approved by President Eisenhower. Even the Russians helped the flood-ravaged people of the area through contributions from the Russian Red Cross and Red Crescent.

The fact that three hurricanes rolled through North Carolina within six weeks was only one of the distinctions of the 1955 season. Remarkably, during this same period, Tampico, Mexico, was also struck by three hurricanes. In the space of twenty-five days, Gladys, Hilda, and Janet all sliced across the Yucatan Peninsula and onto the beaches near Tampico. Hurricane Janet was a rare category-five cyclone that brought great death and destruction to every location it touched. Janet's winds reached 175–200 mph during portions of its trek across the western Caribbean and Gulf of Mexico. Weather Bureau officials reported that when Janet struck Mexico, "the resulting floods culminated in the greatest natural catastrophe in the history of that country."

The 1955 hurricane season was like no other. Gordon Dunn, chief forecaster for the Weather Bureau in Miami, reported that "for the second con-

secutive year, all records were broken for hurricane destruction." And the storms that rolled through Hurricane Alley were responsible for a large part of the trouble.

HELENE (SEPTEMBER 27, 1958)

Perhaps the most intense tropical storm to threaten the Carolina coast during the fifties was hurricane Helene. Helene passed just twenty miles offshore and barely missed the Cape Fear region on the morning of September 27, 1958. Earlier, the storm had charted a course directly toward the Tar Heel coastline. But fortunately, Helene veered away not a moment too soon, sparing a direct hit near Southport. Also, its approach coincided with low tide, subtracting from the potential flooding it could have delivered.

Even though Helene's most powerful energies remained at sea, new wind records were established at several locations near the coast. At Bluenthal Airport in Wilmington, gusts of 135 mph were recorded, eclipsing the old mark for that station. An observer near Southport estimated winds at 125 mph and gusts to 150–60 mph. Barometric pressures hovered around 27.75 inches, and 8 to 10 inches of rain were dumped along the coast. Helene might have been a more intense storm than Hazel, but because it never made landfall and arrived at low tide, flooding was moderate. Nevertheless, damage to the state was estimated at $11 million.

At Southport, wind damage was significant, and overall destruction was said to have been greater than Hazel in '54. Long Beach suffered as well, when overwash covered roads with sand in some areas and undermined them in others. Nine cottages lost their roofs, and virtually every structure on the island received some damage.

At Wrightsville Beach, a member of the Weather Bureau staff made a careful swell count on the morning the hurricane arrived. Incredibly, Helene produced only two and a half to three giant swells per minute. This report was described as "probably the lowest count ever recorded for the area and indicates a storm of exceptional intensity." Overall, however, tides along the ocean beaches were only three to five feet above normal.

Five thousand residents evacuated their homes from Calabash to Morehead City. Almost all of the reported damages were the result of powerful, gusting winds. Crops were blown down in the fields, and roofs suffered greatly as far north as Cedar Island. Helene would have been even more destructive if its intense northeastern quadrant had moved over the Outer Banks.

Governor Hodges, by this time keenly experienced in hurricane disasters, drove into Wilmington just before Helene passed by. About one hundred residents had refused to be evacuated from Carolina and Kure Beaches, and there was great fear that they might be lost to the storm. Governor Hodges tried to make a television appeal to the remaining beach residents, but he never went on the air. The television station lost power before he could broadcast his plea. Eventually, the governor and his party drove to Wrightsville Beach, where they rode out the storm in a shelter on Johnny Mercer's pier.

No deaths were attributed to Helene in North Carolina, and only a few minor injuries were reported. One woman in Jacksonville was injured when a tree fell through her mobile home, striking her on the head. Few injuries or problems resulted from the storm, because evacuations of vulnerable areas were very complete and cooperation among agencies was well tuned. One official noted, "We were prepared for Helene. You might say that we've had lots of recent experience, with Hazel and Diane, and we knew what to look for."

DONNA (SEPTEMBER 11, 1960)

In the years following the string of hurricane tragedies of the fifties, residents all along the Atlantic coast kept watchful eyes on the storms that brewed during each hurricane season. Storm tracking and forecasting was improving, and hurricane warnings were becoming more reliable. The advent of television helped many residents stay informed about approaching storms. Late in the summer of 1960 the people of eastern North Carolina watched cautiously as another dangerous cyclone raced across the Atlantic and headed toward Florida. This new storm left heavy destruction and scores of dead in its wake

Hurricane Donna struck North Carolina in September 1960, leaving coastal residents with the familiar task of storm cleanup. (Photo courtesy of the News and Observer Publishing Co./ N.C. Division of Archives and History)

Although Donna was one of the most powerful hurricanes of the century when it ripped across Florida as a category four, it arrived in North Carolina as a category three, still potent enough to demolish this block home on Atlantic Beach. (Photo courtesy of Roy Hardee)

Marines from Camp Lejeune use heavy equipment to rebuild lost dunes at Atlantic Beach after hurricane Donna. (Photo courtesy of Carteret County Historical Society)

even before it reached the United States. It then went on to become one of the most potent hurricanes in history. Its name was Donna.

Early in September, hurricane Donna developed from a tropical wave that moved westward from the Cape Verde Islands off of the African coast. On September 4, it swept over the Leeward Islands and then bounced along the northern coast of Puerto Rico. Before it passed by the Cuban coast on September 7, Donna had already claimed more than 120 lives. As it turned its sights on southern Florida, this monster hurricane packed winds in excess of 150 mph. On September 9, 1960, Donna blasted the Florida Keys with a thirteen-foot storm surge and deadly winds that gusted between 175 and 200 mph. Its barometric pressure dropped to 27.46 inches, making it one of the most intense hurricanes of the century. Several spans of the famous ocean causeway that extended from Key Largo to Key West were washed away by the violent seas. The destruction throughout this region was the worst since the Labor Day Hurricane of 1935.

As Donna crossed into the Gulf of Mexico in the early hours of September 10, its fickle character became evident when it abruptly turned ninety degrees to the north. From that point, the storm slammed into the Florida coast for a second time, striking near Fort Myers, on the Gulf shore. Donna then crossed the state on a northeast track and moved back into the Atlantic near Daytona Beach. Along the way, it brought record destruction to Florida, including heavy damages to the state's citrus crop. In all, thirteen lives were lost in the

Children sleep in the hallway of the Morehead City Town Hall as Donna's eye passes directly over them. Many public facilities were transformed into shelters during hurricane emergencies. (Photo courtesy of Roy Hardee)

The overwash that struck this western section of Atlantic Beach during hurricane Donna left deep sand in the streets and fractured houses all around. (Photo courtesy of Roy Hardee)

Donna left debris throughout the streets of Swansboro.

Sunshine state. But Donna's escapades did not end with its journey through Florida. By the afternoon of September 10, the hurricane was positioned off the Georgia coast, where it regained much of its strength from the warm waters of the Gulf Stream.

Late in the evening of September 11, Donna moved across the North Carolina coastline near Topsail Island. Winds gusted in excess of 100 mph, and tides ran four to eight feet above normal. Wilmington reported a peak gust of 97 mph, but winds at several locations along the Outer Banks were higher.

The eastern overwash at Atlantic Beach struck the Dunes Club head on, ripping the structure apart and carrying portions of its floor and roof across Fort Macon Road. The overwash was later filled in, the roadway restored, and the Dunes Club rebuilt.

Donna continued on a northeasterly course, passing over Carteret, Pamlico, Hyde, and Tyrrell Counties before crossing over Albemarle Sound and through Elizabeth City. Eventually, it returned to the Atlantic for the second time near Virginia Beach on the morning of September 12.

Coastal communities from Carolina Beach to Nags Head suffered extensive structural damage. Beach erosion was severe in some locations, and numerous overwashed areas were reported. Wind damage was severe, especially to crops, as far as fifty miles inland. Numerous trees were toppled, and power outages were typical along the coast.

The Morehead City–Beaufort causeway after hurricane Donna.

Several motorists became trapped in the rapidly rising tides that swept over the Morehead City–Beaufort causeway during hurricane Donna and were forced to seek higher ground, leaving their automobiles behind.

Carteret County found itself on the eastern side of the storm, and the coastal communities of Atlantic Beach, Morehead City, and Beaufort were among the hardest hit. In Atlantic Beach, several buildings were leveled, including a pavilion and a bakery constructed of concrete block. Numerous structures lost their roofs completely, and many decks and porches were ripped away by high winds. Donna's storm tide cut through the protective dune line in several places, overwashing streets and undermining homes. Breakers ripped through the dunes on Knollwood Drive in Pine Knoll Shores, and a second overwash carried away a twenty-five-foot section of Ocean Ridge

Donna's track northward brought flooding to downtown Manteo. (Photo courtesy of the Outer Banks History Center)

The Dare Hardware Company in Manteo was wrecked during hurricane Donna. (Photo courtesy of the Outer Banks History Center)

Donna destroyed the Waterfront Theater near Manteo, home of The Lost Colony. (Photo by Aycock Brown; courtesy of the Outer Banks History Center)

Across eastern North Carolina, countless trees were downed during hurricane Donna. Many fell on power lines, cars, houses, and other structures. This large pine fell into a home near Jacksonville.

Road in Atlantic Beach. But perhaps the most impressive overwash occurred just east of the Oceanna Pier, where the Dunes Club was destroyed. The beach club was broken apart by the waves, and the main floor of the structure was washed onto Fort Macon Road. The roadway was undermined as well, isolating the Coast Guard station and all points east of the overwash.

Some of the heaviest destruction in the Carteret region occurred on the Morehead City–Beaufort Causeway along a low-lying stretch of Highway 70. This area had been hard hit during Hazel, and Donna's winds and tides brought even greater destruction. After the hurricane had passed, reporters flocked to the scene, and one writer for the *Greensboro Daily News* described the aftermath:

> Up and down the causeway almost everything is wreckage. Power and telephone lines are down across the road, the poles snapped off at their bases. The road itself is half-gone in spots, thick chunks of broken asphalt just out of the pits and ravines carved into the sand by the wind-driven tides. The Beaufort and Morehead Railroad runs in a single track along the north side of the causeway, and it is here that Donna did the railroad dirty. The storm cut the sand from under the tracks and left the crossties hanging — barely in some places — by the rail spikes, and the rails themselves dangling over the water like two long strands of half-cooked spaghetti. A diesel engine leans crazily toward the water — still on the tracks, but with nowhere to go. Behind it, on both sides of what used to be the railroad embankment, stretches a bizarre parade of upturned boats, beds, tables, pillows, smashed planking, pilings, beams and driftwood. A pair of water skis, a child's doll, an outboard motor housing, a sofa that got out of its house without, somehow, making a hole in either wall, windows or door.

At the height of the storm, an ambulance was swept off the causeway by the tide. Driver Bert Brooks and his companion, Cecil Moore, were transporting Annie White to the Morehead City hospital. White was expecting a baby and was being taken there for fear that the hurricane might isolate her from the mainland. The rapidly rising tide caught the ambulance before Brooks and his passengers could make their way across the bridge. They emerged from the vehicle in chest-deep water and managed to retreat to a house on the causeway, where they were able to safely ride out the storm. The ambulance was badly damaged and was partially buried in the sand. Annie White didn't have her baby that night after all, but gave birth two weeks later.

The Outer Banks were struck with the full fury of Donna. High winds, estimated to be 120 mph in some locations, ripped away roofs and toppled miles of telephone and power lines. The storm's early southeast winds piled a mass of water up the Pamlico, Albemarle, and Currituck Sounds, inundating their banks and tributary rivers. As the hurricane passed, the winds turned to the

This car was almost flattened by the collapse of a large tree near Kinston. (Photo courtesy of the News and Observer Publishing Co./N.C. Division of Archives and History)

northeast and a raging flood struck the Outer Banks. Dozens of homes on the soundside of Kitty Hawk and Nags Head were severely damaged. At least three houses were swept into Roanoke Sound near the Little Bridge between Nags Head and Manteo. Violet Kellam, owner of the Oasis Restaurant at the Little Bridge, escaped as her business collapsed around her. She told the *Virginian-Pilot* that "the water rose more than three feet in 15 minutes" and the eye lasted "more than an hour." In some areas, it was reported that "telephone poles popped like firecrackers."

Dozens of towns and cities in the east suffered damages from hurricane Donna. In New Bern, many large trees were downed, and some crashed into homes and businesses. In Washington, Edenton, Swan Quarter, and Elizabeth City, fallen trees and toppled power lines were reported, as well as water damage. More than seventy miles of power lines were downed north of Swan Quarter, and most communities in the northeastern counties were without electricity. Donna's ferocious winds also reached inland and struck signs, trees, and telephone poles in Kinston, Goldsboro, and Greenville. Two tornadoes were observed during the storm, one in Bladen County and one in Sampson County.

Like so many other great hurricanes, Donna didn't end its journey by fizzling out over the Atlantic. Instead, it maintained its course toward New England and struck Long Island, New York, later in the day on September 12. There the storm delivered a ten-foot storm surge and caused extensive damage. Block Island, Rhode Island, recorded sustained winds of 95 mph, with gusts up to 130 mph. Damage was reported all along the northeast coast, from Virginia to Maine. Donna eventually weakened when it crossed the Gulf of St. Lawrence on a northerly track.

Hurricane Donna caused a record amount of destruction in Florida and brought significant damage to the storm-weary residents of eastern North Carolina. By hitting New England with a powerful blow, Donna became a menacing oddity—it was the first storm to strike with hurricane-force winds in Florida, the Carolinas, and New England within the seventy-five-year record of the Weather Bureau. Damage estimates in the United States topped $426 million, although Donna's total cost was believed to be more than $1 billion. At least 50 deaths were blamed on the storm in the United States, and 121 lives were lost in the Caribbean.

In North Carolina, there were eight deaths. Three boys drowned when they took refuge in a house that was swept away by the tide. One person was electrocuted by a fallen power line, and two died when they were crushed by large trees that crashed into their homes. Two others were killed in weather-related traffic accidents. Over one hundred injuries were reported across the state.

Donna's arrival in North Carolina just a few short years after Hazel and the other major storms of the fifties was difficult for many coastal residents to take. But very few packed up and moved away from their homes near the shore. In an editorial that appeared in the *Carteret County News-Times* shortly after the storm, the editor summarized the mood of the local people: "Donna left in her wake not only material destruction but crushed spirits. You can fight just so many hurricanes and then the loss of your business, home, plus the drudgery of back-breaking clean-up begins to be a heart-breaking task. Carteret will come back, because there's nothing else to do but that, but the novelty of hurricanes has long worn off."

In the years following the hurricane tragedies of Hazel, Connie, Diane, Ione, and Donna, the coastal waters of North Carolina remained relatively quiet. Several tropical storms and hurricanes passed east of Hatteras, but for more than a decade no substantial hurricane destruction occurred in the state. This mysterious period of calm was a blessing to the many coastal residents who had repaired and rebuilt their homes and businesses after Donna. This period was also one of unprecedented growth along the coast. Numerous beachfront communities prospered as they became widely recognized as major tourist destinations.

THE MODERN ERA, 1960–1993

Track of hurricane Ginger, 1971

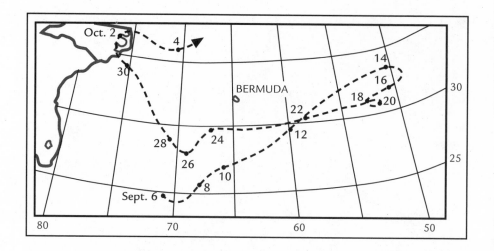

GINGER (SEPTEMBER 30–OCTOBER 1, 1971)

Hurricane Ginger was the first hurricane in several years to test the will of North Carolina's coastal residents. On September 30, 1971, Ginger made landfall on Atlantic Beach as a mild category-one storm. Gusts were reported as high as 92 mph in Atlantic Beach, 70 mph at Cape Hatteras, and 58 mph at Topsail Beach. Tides along the beaches were about four feet above normal, although several locations along the banks of Pamlico Sound recorded tides of five to seven feet.

Rainfall from Ginger was heavy, largely because of the extremely slow movement of the storm. Rainfall totals greater than ten inches were reported at Bayboro, Belhaven, Aurora, and Roanoke Island. The combined effects of heavy rains and wind brought damage to thousands of acres of corn, soybeans, and other crops. The total losses to agriculture alone were estimated at $10 million.

Property damages along the coast were relatively minor. Some trees were uprooted, some power lines downed, and numerous mobile homes overturned. Television aerials, signs, and fences were blown down, and dozens of plate-glass shop windows were shattered. Thousands evacuated oceanfront beaches and low-lying areas and took shelter in schools and other public buildings. Fortunately, Ginger caused no deaths or injuries.

Although Ginger was not as severe as the hurricanes of the fifties, the storm did establish a new weather record—it was the longest-lived hurricane in National Weather Service history. After forming just east of the Bahamas, Ginger moved well to the east of Bermuda and then backtracked toward the Atlantic coast. It was tracked for thirty-one days, during twenty of which it maintained hurricane strength. By the time the storm moved into North Carolina,

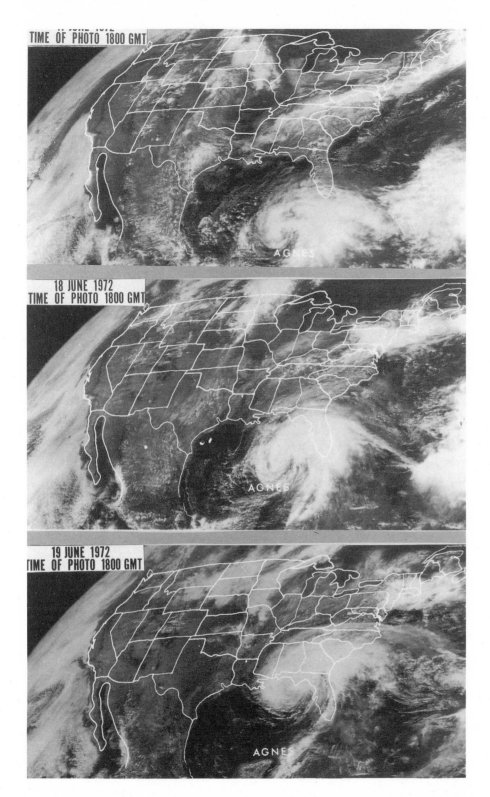

TIME OF PHOTO 1800 GMT

18 JUNE 1972
TIME OF PHOTO 1800 GMT

19 JUNE 1972
TIME OF PHOTO 1800 GMT

AGNES

The broad, spiralling storm clouds of hurricane Agnes dominate these satellite images of the United States. Although Agnes made landfall near Panama City, Florida, it moved northward through the Carolinas, where it combined with a secondary low from the West to produce record floods. (Photos courtesy of the National Weather Service)

it had dissipated substantially. On October 2, Ginger passed over Virginia and out to sea as a weak depression.

AGNES (JUNE 20-21, 1972)

After Ginger crossed the coast in 1971, there was another relatively quiet period along the North Carolina beaches. Few severe storms threatened the state through the remainder of the 1970s. Most of those that did approach were either weak tropical storms or hurricanes that passed far off the coast.

One exception was hurricane Agnes, which moved through the interior portions of Florida, Georgia, and the Carolinas in June 1972. Agnes did have a severe effect on North Carolina, but it was not the coastal region that suffered. Record rainfall occurred on the eastern slopes of the Blue Ridge Mountains from the Carolinas through Virginia. These heavy rains, which totaled more than ten inches in some locations, brought flash floods to mountain and Piedmont streams and major river flooding across the Tar Heel state. The most severe flooding occurred on the Yadkin–Pee Dee River system and on the Dan River. Extensive flooding also occurred along the Catawba, Saluda, Rock, Congaree, Lumber, and Broad Rivers.

Two deaths were blamed on Agnes in North Carolina. One Iredell County man was swept off his tractor by raging floodwaters, and another life was lost when a canoe overturned in Surry County. Damages in the state were estimated at $4.28 million. But the destruction that occurred from Florida to New York made hurricane Agnes one of the most expensive storms in history. Devastating floods in Virginia, Maryland, West Virginia, Pennsylvania, New Jersey, and New York combined with the destruction of fifteen tornadoes in Florida to raise the price tag for Agnes to well over $2 billion. In all, 122 lives were lost in the United States.

DAVID (SEPTEMBER 5, 1979)

In September 1979, hurricane David swept across North Carolina on a track toward the northeastern states. Like Agnes, David moved through the Piedmont, never actually making landfall on the North Carolina coast. David did, however, bring gusting winds and high tides to the southern beaches, as well as heavy rains to numerous locations.

David's greatest destruction occurred before the storm reached the continent. More than one thousand deaths were blamed on the hurricane as it passed through the Caribbean Sea. Winds of 150 mph lashed Puerto Rico and the Dominican Republic, and heavy rains delivered massive floods to these islands. David's next move was toward the east coast of Florida, where residents in Miami braced for the storm. On Labor Day, September 3, David wobbled erratically, just missed Miami, and struck near Palm Beach. The cyclone then bounced back to sea near Cape Canaveral, Florida, and made landfall again near Savannah, Georgia. From there the hurricane lost much of its energy and passed through central South Carolina and North Carolina as a tropical storm.

Beach erosion was severe along the southern strands of North Carolina, especially in Brunswick County, where most beaches lost thirty to forty feet of sand. At least half a dozen fishing piers were crippled by the storm. Tides were generally three to five feet above normal, although some locations along the banks of Pamlico Sound reported tides of seven feet. Wind gusts of 60 mph were reported at Wrightsville Beach, 54 mph at New River, 53 mph at Atlantic Beach, 43 mph at Cape Hatteras, and 36 mph in Raleigh. Rainfall over several eastern counties ranged from seven to ten inches.

In Goldsboro, tornado-like winds toppled trees in the downtown area. Town employees in Belhaven were forced to evacuate when five inches of water sloshed inside Town Hall. About thirty thousand Carolina Power and Light customers were without electricity when gusting winds pitched tree limbs into power lines. Seven eastern North Carolina counties closed their schools because of the threat of flooded highways. Fortunately, no deaths or injuries were reported in the state.

David continued to deliver heavy rains and gusting winds to the Northeast after the storm passed through the Carolinas on September 6. Virginia, Maryland, Pennsylvania, New York, Connecticut, and Massachusetts were all hit hard by the storm. Numerous tornadoes were spawned on David's northern track, and three twisters caused deaths in Philadelphia, southern New Jersey, and Rhode Island. Throughout its trek of some five thousand miles, hurricane David was responsible for over 1,100 deaths and $2 billion in damages. Like hurricanes Diane in 1955 and Agnes in 1972, David demonstrated the destructive power these storms can possess long after they have tracked inland.

DIANA (SEPTEMBER 9–14, 1984)

Emergency management teams and local officials put their disaster plans into high gear when hurricane Diana approached the North Carolina coast in September 1984. Diana was a fickle storm that finally made landfall near Bald Head Island on September 13 after drifting around Cape Fear for almost two days. Although it had been a minimal category-four storm, Diana was barely a category two by the time it hit the beaches of Brunswick and New Hanover Counties. Nevertheless, it was the first significant hurricane to strike the North Carolina coast since Donna in 1960. The span of time between Donna

Hurricane Diana, the first hurricane to cause significant damage on the North Carolina coast since Donna in 1960, finally made landfall near Bald Head Island in September 1984. This house at Holden Beach was destroyed during the storm. (Photo courtesy of the National Weather Service)

2130Z 11 SEPTEMBER 1984

This late afternoon satellite image of Diana clearly shows the storm's eye poised just off the coast of Cape Fear. The hurricane stalled for more than two days before finally moving onshore. (Photo courtesy of the National Weather Service)

and Diana had been one of the least active in the state's recent hurricane history. As a result, a whole new generation of coastal residents had their first hurricane experience.

Diana began as a small tropical low just north of the Bahama Islands on September 8. By September 10, the low had developed into the first hurricane of the season and was drifting northward about two hundred miles off the Georgia coast. Over the next two days, Diana intensified significantly as it appeared to follow the Gulf Stream toward North Carolina. On September 12, the storm's central pressure reached its lowest value, 28.02 inches. Poised less

than fifty miles off Cape Fear, Diana churned the ocean with sustained winds of 135 mph. At that point it appeared that landfall was imminent and that great destruction would follow.

Hurricane warnings had been issued prior to Diana's approach, and barrier island residents from Myrtle Beach to Ocracoke boarded their homes and evacuated. Thousands took refuge in hotels, schools, and other public shelters. Across the southern coast, residents watched vigilantly as local television newscasters provided around-the-clock updates on the hurricane's movements. But as Diana neared the Cape Fear region, it stalled and wobbled briefly away from land. Some evacuees became impatient after the first night away from their homes and actually returned to the beaches while Diana drifted about. But after some thirty hours, the hesitant hurricane turned and finally made landfall, forcing many to flee for the second time in two days. One Wrightsville Beach resident commented after the storm: "I'm not sure which was worse—the anxiety of worrying about what was going to happen, or the actual storm itself. At least it's over!"

While Diana sat offshore, the once-powerful hurricane lost much of its strength. The highest sustained winds measured on land were 115 mph at the Oak Island Coast Guard station. This report was made on September 11, long before the time of landfall. When the storm did finally move onshore sometime after midnight on September 13, sustained winds were around 92 mph. Gusts throughout the local area surpassed 100 mph.

Fortunately, Diana's stalled movements caused it to weaken, but the timing of its final approach also turned out to be a blessing to beachfront property owners. Landfall occurred very near the time of low tide, and the effects of

Diana toppled many large trees in Brunswick and New Hanover Counties, including this oak in Southport.

Diana's winds buffeted Carolina Beach and caused significant damage to some structures. (Photo courtesy of S. M. Rogers Jr./U.N.C. Sea Grant)

Anne Donnell of Southport searches through the debris in her living room after enduring a frightening visit from hurricane Diana. The storm's gusting winds ripped away a portion of the roof of the Donnell home.

storm surge were minimal. Beach erosion was somewhat severe from the pounding northeast winds, but the storm tide at Carolina Beach was only about five and a half feet. Freshwater flooding was widespread, due to heavy rainfall over a three-day period. Some locations recorded 15.50 inches. The National Weather Service office in Wilmington reported 13.72 inches from September 11 to 14. Dam failures resulted from the torrential rains in Boiling Springs Lake (Brunswick County), Roseboro (Sampson County), and Faison (Duplin County).

The eye of hurricane Diana passed slowly over Southport around 2:00 A.M., after several hours of punishing winds. An eerie calm came over the town as the winds died. While the eye was over Southport it was reported that crickets could be heard chirping in the still night air. Old-timers who could remember the passage of Hazel said there was little comparison; Hazel's eye swept through in only minutes, while Diana's lasted for almost two hours.

Diana weakened quickly after moving onshore and tracked to the northeast as a tropical storm, exiting the coast near Oregon Inlet. Although Brunswick and New Hanover Counties were hardest hit, Pender, Sampson, Bladen, and Columbus Counties also suffered from the storm. A single tornado was reported in Nash County as the remnants of the hurricane returned to sea.

There was widespread tree damage along the coast and in the interior sections near the storm's path. Many large pines and oaks were snapped by gusting winds, but more commonly trees were uprooted and toppled. Heavy rains loosened the soil supporting many trees, aiding their collapse. Downed trees often crashed into homes, blocked streets and highways, and tangled power lines. As a result, some areas were without electricity for days after the storm passed.

Structural damage was widespread but variable. Many newer homes constructed to meet more modern building codes fared well in the storm. Older structures suffered greater damages, including complete roof failures in some cases. In one spectacular incident at Carolina Beach, a large section of roof from a motel flew more than five hundred feet over several buildings, finally crashing into the roof of another two-story structure. Some coastal properties were reportedly "sandblasted enough to damage or remove the paint." In all, the Red Cross estimated that fewer than one hundred homes were completely destroyed, around six hundred were severely damaged, and about "90 percent of the homes touched by the storm received only minor damage."

Agricultural damages from Diana were greatest to corn, soybeans, peanuts, and sweet potatoes. Although total crop losses were near $25 million, the damages were reported to be far less than the crop destruction from the tornadoes that moved through the state in March of the same year. The agricultural damages, when combined with the property losses, brought the total cost of the hurricane to near $85 million. But as one official noted, "You have

Atlantic Beach residents line up at the town hall to be issued their official evacuation reentry passes prior to the arrival of hurricane Gloria in 1985. (Photo courtesy of the Carteret County News-Times*)*

The passage of hurricane Gloria in September 1985 caused significant pier damage along the coast, but overall damage in North Carolina was less than had been expected. The storm caused about $8 million in losses to the state, but well over $1 billion in damages to the Northeast. (Photo courtesy of the Carteret County News-Times*)*

to realize that this could have been far, far worse. This total amounts to small potatoes when compared to other recent hurricanes."

Three deaths were attributed to Diana in North Carolina. One person suffered a fatal heart attack while preparing for the storm, and two died in automobile accidents on water-covered roads. One of those was Brunswick County social services director Larry Bell, who was attempting to make his way to the evacuation shelter he had earlier established.

Diana's impact on North Carolina was not as catastrophic as the impact of the hurricanes of the fifties, and the losses were not nearly as great. Those residents along the southern coast who suffered damages were nevertheless awed by the storm's destructive power. But ironically, this hurricane provided some practical benefits. Coastal communities and state officials were given the opportunity to fully implement their newly developed strategies for mass evacuation and disaster management. In Carteret County, for example, evacuations gave officials a "dry run" that enabled them to make improvements in their plans. And Diana offered the first real wind-effect test of the state's recently modified building codes. Most important, as the first hurricane to strike in many years, Diana delivered a wake-up call to many of North Carolina's coastal residents. They were reminded of the potential for disaster that can be swept ashore with a major storm.

This air-supported phosphate storage building at the state port in Morehead City collapsed from the early morning winds of hurricane Gloria. (Photo courtesy of the Carteret County News-Times*)*

Motorists leaving the Outer Banks crowd the Wright Memorial Bridge before the arrival of hurricane Gloria. (Photo courtesy of the Carteret County News-Times*)*

GLORIA (SEPTEMBER 26–27, 1985)

One year after Diana visited the Cape Fear coast, hurricane Gloria sped toward North Carolina and presented another serious threat to the state. Gloria was a larger, more powerful storm, which appeared to be headed for a direct hit near Cape Lookout. Some had even dubbed it "one of the storms of the century." But like many hurricanes, Gloria changed course slightly as it approached the state and crossed the Outer Banks near Cape Hatteras on September 27, 1985.

Gloria was first observed as a tropical depression off the western coast of Africa on September 15. For several days, the storm drifted across the Atlantic and intensified. On September 22, Gloria reached hurricane strength and began a northwesterly course toward the Carolinas. By the time it reached a point four hundred miles southeast of Cape Hatteras, Gloria's central pressure had dropped below twenty-eight inches. For the second time in two years, a category-four hurricane was threatening North Carolina's beaches.

Hurricane warnings were issued, and thousands fled their homes to seek refuge in emergency shelters. Schools, hospitals, churches, and other public facilities were packed with evacuees, just as they had been during Diana. But the warnings for Gloria were more ominous and the evacuations more complete. Even longtime residents of Ocracoke, accustomed to frequent storms and severe hurricanes in the past, left their island homes for safe shelter. Many boarded the ferry to Swan Quarter, where they found refuge in shelters and hotels. It was estimated that less than ninety residents remained on Ocracoke to ride out the storm.

Early predictions called for Gloria to make landfall near Morehead City. But as the hurricane approached the central coast, it swerved northward and passed over Hatteras Island around 1:30 A.M. on September 27. Gloria's eye continued across the banks and reentered the Atlantic near Nags Head on a northeasterly track. From there, the storm regained strength and picked up forward speed. Gloria was moving about 35 mph when it struck the continent for the second time on Long Island, New York. It continued across Long Island Sound and blasted Connecticut, Rhode Island, Massachusetts, and Maine with high winds and heavy rains.

Amazingly, Gloria's sweep of the Outer Banks brought modest damage to the islands. Even though the hurricane had been touted as "the most powerful in years," several factors contributed to the less-than-expected destruction. Fortunately, the lunar tide was receding as the storm brushed over Cape Hatteras. And as with many hurricanes, Gloria's more powerful eastern half remained over the Atlantic as it spun up the coast. Also, Gloria moved through rapidly, never lingering to pile up water and destruction.

Although reconnaissance aircraft had reported winds up to 130 mph, the highest winds measured on land were substantially less. Diamond Shoals Tower, about fifteen miles southeast of Cape Hatteras, recorded maximum sustained winds of 98 mph and gusts to 120 mph. At the Cape Hatteras Weather Station, sustained winds of 74 mph and gusts to 86 mph were measured. Several locations from Ocracoke to Virginia Beach reported gusts over 100 mph. But overall, Gloria's winds were less than had been expected.

Observers at the Cape Hatteras Weather Station recorded a low pressure reading of 27.98 inches, classifying Gloria as a category-three storm at the time of landfall. As the Weather Service staff anxiously watched their radar screens and instruments, the hurricane's eight-mile-wide eye rolled directly over the station. The storm's howling winds dropped quickly to 6 mph, and the calm lasted for about thirty-seven minutes. But when the southern eye wall struck, it hit quickly, and the light winds grew to hurricane force within three minutes. The rapid changes in barometric pressure that occurred with the passing of Gloria's eye caused headaches and "popping" ears in the Weather Service staff.

High tides were most severe along the northern Outer Banks. Highway 12 was overwashed in several locations, and sand covered the roadway near Avon and on the northern end of Ocracoke. Tides were generally six to eight feet above normal on the Outer Banks, six feet in the Cherry Point area, and four feet at Wrightsville Beach. Erosion along the oceanfront was severe in numerous locations, as some beaches lost more than twenty-five feet of dune. Rainfall totals included 7.80 inches at Williamston, 7.09 inches at New Bern, and 7.00 inches at Cherry Point. Although the hurricane tracked directly over the island, Cape Hatteras reported only 2.10 inches.

Dare County suffered the greatest damages from hurricane Gloria. In Manteo, four feet of water flooded downtown streets and several businesses. Two fires blazed out of control on Roanoke Island during the storm. A home on Pond Island, near Manteo, was lost when firefighters were forced to retreat as floodwaters rose. A dangling power line was believed responsible for another fire at the Ace Hardware store on Highway 64. Firemen battling the blaze lost their water supply and were forced to pump water out of nearby flooded streets. By daybreak the store had been leveled.

As with most hurricanes, high winds caused thousands to lose power during the storm. Trees were uprooted, mobile homes were flipped over, and several structures lost their roofs. Numerous fishing piers were damaged by the storm's rolling seas. The double-masted cargo schooner *Jens Juhl* broke from its moorings near Beaufort and snapped its masts as it became wedged under a nearby drawbridge. In Morehead City, high winds ripped open an air-supported phosphate storage building at the state port. Residents were surprised to see the "balloon building" deflated in the aftermath of Gloria.

But the damage in North Carolina from Gloria totaled only about $8 million, far less than expected. In an interview with the *News and Observer* after the storm, state emergency management official Lt. Douglas Hoell Jr. commented on Gloria's toll: "We were amazed at the lack of damage for a storm this size. We're concerned that people are going to look at this hurricane and say this was the fourth worst hurricane ever, and it didn't do any damage. So they may not evacuate next time, and next time may be the killer storm." Only one death was attributed to Gloria in North Carolina, when a tree fell into a mobile home and killed a man.

After Gloria brushed by the Carolina coast, it maintained its course and

As hurricane Charley passes nearby, a Beaufort resident bails out his boat on the waterfront at Taylor's Creek. (Photo courtesy of Scott Taylor)

slammed into the waterfront communities of Long Island, New York. From there the storm passed over Connecticut and sped through central New England, finally dissipating over Canada. Over one million residents were without electricity throughout the region, as 100- to 130-mph gusts ripped down power lines and trees and battered homes. Several tornadoes were spawned as the hurricane tracked over one of the most densely populated regions of the country. At least six deaths were blamed on Gloria in the Northeast, and damages surpassed $1 billion on Long Island alone. Much like the Great Atlantic Hurricane of 1944, Gloria had swept the Outer Banks and then the New England states within just a matter of hours.

Gloria's impact on North Carolina was not significant, but like Diana the year before, it caught the undivided attention of the state's coastal residents. And like so many storms before it, Gloria punished the Outer Banks more severely than other parts of the Carolina coast. Fortunately, its passage left few scars on the Tar Heel state.

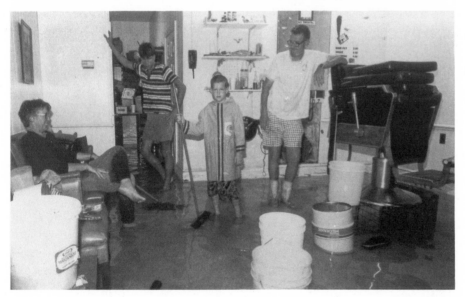

CHARLEY (AUGUST 17–18, 1986)

Hurricane Charley put North Carolina's emergency evacuation plans to a test
when it abruptly crossed the Outer Banks on a busy summer weekend in 1986.
Charley originated in the eastern Gulf of Mexico as a tropical depression on
August 12. By the fifteenth, the storm had crossed southern Georgia and entered the Atlantic off the coast of Savannah. Then, on August 17, the depression rapidly intensified and threatened the beaches of North Carolina.

Unlike the more powerful Cape Verde–type hurricanes that may be ob-

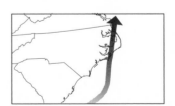

served for thousands of miles before they reach land, Charley sprang up quickly and caught residents and officials off guard. Very little lead time was available to prepare evacuation shelters or implement emergency plans. One official with the National Weather Service summarized Charley's approach: "It was sitting off the coast of South Carolina as a small low pressure area and then almost explosively, it became a hurricane."

Fortunately, as Charley drifted across Ocracoke, Pamlico Sound, Hyde and Dare Counties, and the Currituck area, it was classified as a "weak" category-one hurricane. The storm exited the state through eastern Virginia before losing its hurricane intensity and returning to sea. Charley was a very short lived hurricane, as it only maintained that status for twenty-four hours. Its 75-mph winds delivered minimal damage throughout the region. Land stations reported sustained wind speeds of less than hurricane force, although gusts to 80 mph were recorded in Hyde County and along the northern Outer Banks. Cape Lookout reported gusts to 58 mph; Wilmington's highest wind was only 29 mph. Charley's greatest winds were reported near the Chesapeake Bay Bridge-Tunnel where a gust of 104 mph was recorded.

Because of Charley's rapid approach, and because much of the storm's intensity was gained overnight, residents and vacationers had very little time to prepare. A voluntary evacuation was announced at around 8:00 A.M. on Sunday, August 17, just hours before the storm skipped across the state. About twenty thousand people left coastal areas within those few hours, causing massive traffic snarls along major evacuation routes in the east. Traffic leaving Atlantic Beach and Emerald Isle was backed up in eight-to-twelve-mile lines from the bridges on either end of Bogue Banks. Farther north, traffic on U.S. 158 was, at one point, frozen in a line twenty-five miles long as anxious travelers fled the northern Outer Banks for the mainland.

The mass exodus left many tourists and residents frustrated. Some sat in traffic for more than three hours and only moved a few blocks. Others gave up on their attempts to leave the barrier islands and returned to their homes and hotels after enduring hours of waiting in traffic. Many feared that they might be trapped in their cars when the hurricane struck. But fortunately, Charley's winds and tides did not pose a significant threat to those who fled the storm.

Charley's overall impact on the state was minimal, with light damage reported to trees and power lines. One death was attributed to the storm—a motorist drowned while attempting to cross a flooded causeway near Manteo. The dollar losses from storm damage were not great, although the loss of revenue from abbreviated vacations may have had a significant impact on the summer tourism trade. But most important, hurricane Charley offered lessons in evacuation planning and demonstrated how quickly tropical cyclones can threaten.

Louise Palmer stands in front of her heavily damaged home in Mayesville, S.C., after the passing of hurricane Hugo in September 1989. Even though the storm's most dramatic effects were on the South Carolina coast, inland residents in North and South Carolina were rocked by high winds. (Photo courtesy of the Charlotte Observer*)*

HUGO (SEPTEMBER 21–22, 1989)

Few hurricanes of the modern era have caused greater destruction or loss than hurricane Hugo did in September 1989. Hugo was an intense Cape Verde storm that began as a cluster of innocent thunderclouds off the western coast of Africa. On September 10, these thunderstorms became a depression that, while drifting westward, grew into a tropical storm on the eleventh and a hurricane on the thirteenth. Hugo gradually curved to the west-northwest and

In the days before Hugo made landfall, residents along the North Carolina coast made preparations for a possible strike, including visits to building supply stores, which sold plywood for use as window covers. (Photo by Drew Wilson; courtesy of the Outer Banks History Center)

slowed its forward speed as it approached the Leeward Islands, packing sustained winds of 160 mph and a central pressure of only 27.11 inches.

This impressive storm rolled over Guadeloupe on September 17, St. Croix on the morning of the eighteenth, and Puerto Rico on the evening of the same day. Hugo attained category-five status briefly while over the Atlantic, but as it moved through these island nations, it ranked as a four. Throughout the eastern Caribbean, the destruction was massive. Damage estimates for the region exceeded $2.5 billion, and at least forty-one lives were lost.

After battering Puerto Rico with 130-mph winds, Hugo turned to the northwest and developed a course that would ultimately lead to the Carolina coast. By September 21, the cyclone was churning the waters of the Atlantic just a few hundred miles east of Florida. At 5:00 A.M. that day, the storm's maximum sustained winds were 110 mph, but by 5:00 P.M. they had increased to 135 mph. Hugo had increased in intensity from category two to category four in only twelve hours. This killer storm was gaining strength and presented a serious threat to the southeastern coast.

On September 20, a hurricane watch was issued for the beaches from St. Augustine, Florida, to Cape Hatteras. Residents began to prepare for the possibility of evacuation. On the morning of the twenty-first, a hurricane warning was issued from Fernandina Beach, Florida, to Cape Lookout. Later that day, the warning was extended northward to Oregon Inlet. But instead of swinging northward as expected, Hugo slammed into the central coastline of South Carolina near Charleston around midnight, September 21.

Landfall occurred at Sullivan's Island, several miles north of Charleston. From there the storm swept inland, maintaining its northwesterly course. As Hugo passed through the central part of the state it weakened slightly, although winds were still of hurricane force when its eye passed between Columbia and Sumter. By 6:00 A.M. on September 22, Hugo had diminished to tropical-storm strength. At daybreak, it passed into North Carolina just west of Charlotte and carved a path through Hickory and over the Blue Ridge Mountains. The storm continued to accelerate as it passed through the state and was advancing at 40 mph when it moved into extreme western Virginia. From there, the remnants of Hugo continued through West Virginia, eastern Ohio, and western Pennsylvania. The once-powerful cyclone was tracked for two more days as an extratropical storm as it turned across eastern Canada and into the North Atlantic.

Hugo was the most powerful hurricane to strike the United States in twenty years. Not since hurricane Camille in 1969 had a storm of such intensity made landfall in the United States. Hugo blasted the South Carolina coast with sustained winds of over 130 mph. In Charleston, the highest sustained wind was estimated at 138 mph. A ship anchored in the Sampit River five miles west of Georgetown reported a sustained wind speed of 120 mph. One hundred miles inland, gusts of 99 mph were reported at Columbia and 109 mph at Sumter. At Folly Beach, on the weaker, southern side of the storm, sustained winds of 85 mph were reported.

The storm surge on the South Carolina coast was extreme. The highest tide was near 20 feet at Bull's Bay, just north of Charleston. This storm tide was the highest ever recorded on the East Coast. Tides were reported of 16 feet at McClellanville, 13 feet at Myrtle Beach, 12 feet at Folly Beach, and 10.5 feet at Charleston. A fisherman in McClellanville reportedly rode out the storm aboard his shrimp trawler and was said to have "floated over the roofs of two-story houses." Not surprisingly, the impact on waterfront properties was enormous.

Hugo's tremendous power delivered incredible destruction across South Carolina. Extreme tides and high winds knocked bridges off their pilings, stranded yachts in the middle of highways, and toppled television broadcast towers. The 150-mile-wide swath of the storm was especially devastating to the forests of the state, as more than six billion board feet of timber were destroyed. That total was more than three times the loss experienced with the Mount St. Helens volcanic eruption in 1980. The Francis Marion National Forest just north of Charleston was among the hardest-hit areas. The U.S. Forest Service estimated that Hugo damaged or destroyed 70 percent of the

Massive oaks and other hardwoods were toppled throughout the Charlotte area during hurricane Hugo. Cleanup of the downed trees took many weeks. (Photo courtesy of the Charlotte Observer*)*

Following hurricane Hugo, children stare in amazement at the fallen trees on a neighbor's home in Charlotte. (Photo courtesy of the Charlotte Observer*)*

trees in the 250,000-acre forest, or about one billion board feet of timber. Very few of the uprooted and splintered trees were harvestable, and the economic losses of the timber alone were over $1 billion.

In North Carolina, Hugo had a severe impact, both on the beaches of Brunswick County and in the cities and towns in the western portions of the state. Damage was reported in twenty-nine counties, most of which were designated as federal disaster areas. As the center of the storm rolled past Charlotte, wind gusts of over 85 mph buffeted the region. Trees crashed into homes, cars, and power lines, and utility poles snapped. Charlotte lost more than eighty thousand trees to the storm, many of which were more than seventy years old. Ninety-eight percent of the city's residents lost power, and for some, repairs were not made for more than two weeks. Power outages caused large amounts of raw sewage to bypass treatment plants and flow into streams throughout Mecklenburg County. North Carolina's largest metropolitan area was brought to its knees by the storm.

Numerous other cities and towns felt Hugo's wrath as it crossed the state. Gastonia, Monroe, Lincolnton, and Hickory were all hit hard by the storm. Two to four inches of rain fell across the western counties, although Boone received almost seven inches. High winds ripped down power lines throughout the region, and forests in some areas were leveled. In North Carolina, Hugo damaged more than 2.7 million acres of forests in twenty-six counties, with almost complete destruction of 68,000 acres. Timber losses to the state were valued at $250 million. And like South Carolina, very little timber was sal-

Hugo's effect on a Charlotte home. (Photo by Jane Faircloth; courtesy of Transparencies, Inc.)

vaged. Forestry experts were overwhelmed by the sheer volume of dead trees. Most of the timber was either splintered by the storm or decayed before loggers could reach it.

In the wake of the storm, Tar Heel residents emerged from their homes in awe of the destruction. So many trees, tree limbs, and utility poles were downed that they completely filled the streets and yards of some neighborhoods. Cleanup efforts began almost immediately but were slowed one week after Hugo when seven more inches of rain fell across several western counties. Chainsaws were essential in clearing streets and lawns, but perhaps the most valued commodity in the aftermath of the storm was one we often take for granted—electricity.

From the South Carolina coast to the hollows of the Blue Ridge Mountains, over 1.5 million people were without electric power the morning after the storm. Utility companies scrambled to put crews to work repairing and replacing downed poles and lines. In some areas, the destruction was so extensive that it was difficult to tell where the lines used to be. Line crews, equipment, and supplies were brought in from around the nation to assist with the effort. Some areas were back in service within days, but others were

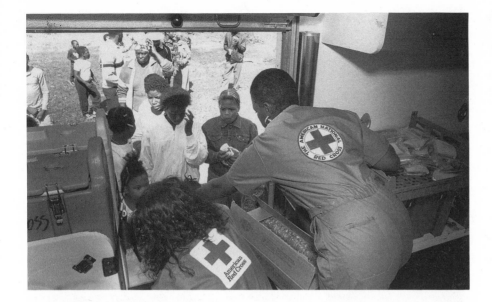

Relief efforts after hurricane Hugo extended through portions of western North Carolina that had been affected by the storm. (Photo courtesy of the Charlotte Observer)

Dare County residents gather food and supplies for shipment to the storm-ravaged victims of hurricane Hugo. (Photo courtesy of the Coastland Times)

without power for weeks. Many crews worked sixteen-hour days and spent weeks away from their families to get the job done. Most residents were appreciative of the line crews' heroic efforts, but tempers sometimes flared as some customers remained in the dark while their neighbors' lights were on.

Duke Power Company was just one utility that reckoned with Hugo's aftermath. In the effort to restore electricity to 700,000 of its customers in North and South Carolina, Duke spent $62.5 million in just two weeks. More than 9,000 workers replaced 8,800 poles, 700 miles of cable and wire, 6,300 transformers, and 1,700 electric meters. The overall recovery effort was unprecedented in North Carolina history. The importance of restoring electricity after any hurricane was highlighted in a government report following Hugo: "In any large-scale natural disaster, energy is the common denominator. Its loss is capable of causing severe economic dislocation. On the other hand, it is essential to recovery as well. In the case of hurricane Hugo, electric power was the principal infrastructure component that had to be rapidly restored. Because the prolonged disruption of electric power can have profound adverse effects on health, safety, commerce and industry, emergency planners must be prepared to respond accordingly."

The southern beaches of the North Carolina coast also suffered from the effects of Hugo. In Brunswick County, the storm produced an eight-to-ten-foot storm surge that battered beachfront cottages. Over 120 homes on Holden Beach, Ocean Isle Beach, and Long Beach were either destroyed or condemned because they suffered extensive damage. Severe beach erosion affected these barrier islands, in many cases washing away the protective dunes that lined their shores. Oceanfront fishing piers were bashed and damaged in Brunswick, New Hanover, Pender, and Onslow Counties. But the most significant of the state's coastal destruction occurred in Brunswick County, where damage estimates topped $75 million.

At the time Hugo struck in 1989, it was the most expensive hurricane in U.S. history. Approximately $10 billion in property was destroyed, $7 billion on the U.S. mainland, $2 billion in Puerto Rico, and $1 billion elsewhere. In North Carolina, the price tag was around $1 billion, even though the storm made landfall in Charleston, some two hundred miles away. As a result, Hugo became the most expensive hurricane in North Carolina history as well.

The total number of deaths associated with the storm was estimated at eighty-two, including seven in North Carolina, twenty-seven in South Carolina, six in Virginia, and one in New York. Several lives were lost during the cleanup efforts, which lasted for months after the storm. Dozens of injuries were reported ranging from severe cuts and broken limbs to heart attacks. Cleanup crews often encountered live power cables, and chainsaw-related injuries were common. But considering the widespread destruction Hugo brought to the Carolinas, the death toll could have been much higher.

Hurricane Hugo was one of the greatest natural disasters to ever affect the United States. Like Hazel, Camille, and a handful of other hurricanes, Hugo didn't lose its punch when it struck the coast but instead barreled inland with almost full fury. The people of Mecklenburg County thought they were immune to hurricanes prior to this storm's arrival. Most had believed that tropical cyclones were strictly a coastal phenomenon, but Hugo proved to be an exception. After breaking all dollar records for destruction, this incredible storm was overshadowed just three years later by another record-breaking hurricane that more than doubled Hugo's toll: hurricane Andrew.

EMILY (AUGUST 31, 1993)

When hurricane Emily staggered toward the North Carolina coast in late August 1993, tourists and residents along the Outer Banks gave careful thought to the call for evacuation. Along with the rest of the nation, they remembered the vivid scenes of destruction left in the wake of two recent national tragedies. Hurricanes Hugo in 1989 and Andrew in 1992 had generated a healthy new respect for these storms, and many vacationers were not about to take any chances. On August 29, 1993, a voluntary evacuation was announced along much of the North Carolina coast. The next day, the National Hurricane Center in Coral Gables, Florida, issued a statement that included a probability forecast: The chance of Emily making landfall between Wilmington and Norfolk was 21 percent or greater.

On Hatteras Island and Ocracoke, officials made a tough call—they ordered a mandatory evacuation, even though Emily was still almost thirty-six hours away. In years past, some evacuation decisions had been decidedly unpopular, causing merchants to lose tourist dollars and vacationers to lose their time on the beach. Resentment often followed when hurricanes changed course and evacuations turned into false alarms.

But as Emily tracked steadily toward the banks, a stream of cars flowed along Highway 12 and off Hatteras Island. On Ocracoke ferries were filled to capacity, carrying tourists and residents to the mainland. The State Highway Patrol estimated that as many as 90 percent of the people on the banks complied with the call for evacuation. Approximately 120,000 people made the move to avoid the storm. It was estimated that only about 1,000 remained on Hatteras Island to greet Emily when it arrived.

When hurricane Bob slashed past the Outer Banks in 1991, some estimates placed the evacuation response at only 50 percent. Officials conceded that the horrifying images of South Florida in the aftermath of Andrew played a role in the increased concern. "There's no doubt about it," declared one Buxton resident. "Hugo and Andrew showed us how bad these things can be. I have no desire to stick around and find out for myself."

Hurricane Emily did eventually brush Hatteras Island around 7:00 P.M. on August 31, striking the area with sustained winds of 92 mph. The storm was by no means comparable to Andrew or Hugo but was instead rated as a minimum category three, with maximum sustained winds of 115 mph. Fortunately, the higher winds remained just offshore, as Emily's thirty-mile-wide eye came within thirteen miles of Cape Hatteras. Nevertheless, the villages of Hatteras, Frisco, Buxton, and Avon were battered by the storm as it bumped northward along the Outer Banks. On the following day, September 1, Emily turned eastward off the Virginia coast and tracked into the cooler waters of the North Atlantic.

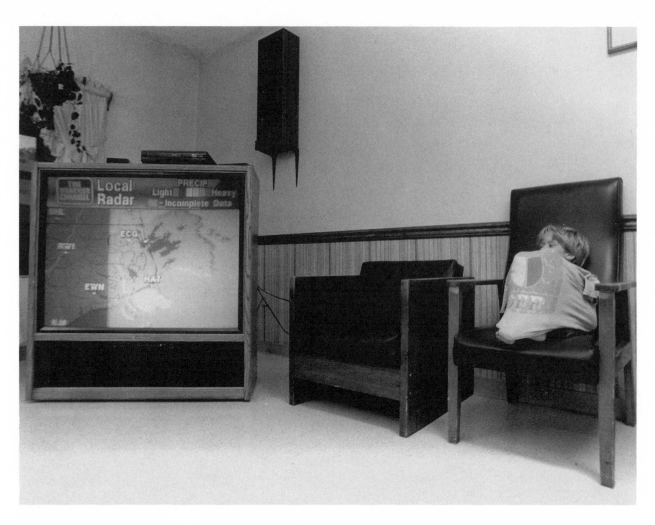

As hurricane Emily churns over the Outer Banks, a frightened young resident of Nags Head studies a radar update. (Photo courtesy of Drew Wilson/Virginian-Pilot/ Carolina Coast)

Although the eye of the storm never actually touched land, Emily's impact on the people and property of the Cape Hatteras area was traumatic. Gusting winds, unofficially clocked at more than 111 mph, snapped ninety-foot pine trees, toppled small buildings, and ripped away roofs. Six Coast Guard family homes in Buxton were leveled by what was at first believed to be a tornado. Later analysis showed that straight, sustained winds had caused the destruction. Mobile homes were rolled over by the blasts of wind, and others had their roofs peeled back "like cans of sardines." One resident watched as a telephone booth rolled off its foundation and into the street.

Most of the major wind damage occurred to older homes or to buildings that were not built to code. The most common structures affected were signboards, porches, poorly connected roofs, eaves, storage sheds, and mobile homes. If Emily had not been deflected by an approaching cold front, landfall might have brought much higher winds and significantly more destruction.

Emily's winds ripped across Pamlico Sound and piled waist-deep water in

The strong winds and high tides that battered the Outer Banks during hurricane Emily were the most severe to strike the region in many years. (Photo courtesy of Drew Wilson/Virginian-Pilot/Carolina Coast)

As with many hurricanes affecting the Outer Banks, Emily's most severe floods came from the rising waters of Pamlico Sound. (Photo courtesy of Drew Wilson/Virginian-Pilot/Carolina Coast)

the streets and homes of several Hatteras Island villages. The flooding was made worse by the occurrence of a full moon, which brought even higher tides to the region. Cars were "floating" in several parking lots in Buxton. In numerous homes, waist-high waves broke through windows and rolled into living rooms. The flooding was about one to two feet higher than predicted on one-hundred-year flood maps, resulting in the need for revised maps for Hatteras Island.

By 7:00 P.M. on August 31, the Dare County Emergency Operations center in Buxton had to be abandoned because of the rising tide. Four feet of water flooded the building, forcing county and local officials to retreat to higher ground. Cape Hatteras School was hard hit by the tide, which filled the hallways and classrooms to a depth of four feet. Among the losses were computers, copiers, and thousands of brand-new textbooks. Total damages at the school alone exceeded $3 million.

Flooding along the shores of Pamlico Sound was about ten and a half feet above normal from just north of Buxton to Avon. At Frisco and Hatteras village, the tide was about eight and a half feet. Along portions of Highway 12, sound waters came within one vertical foot of breaching the oceanfront dunes. Surprisingly, the oceanside storm surge was moderate, breaking through the dunes in two locations south of Frisco.

In the wake of the hurricane, residents of the storm-ravaged areas began the arduous task of cleaning up their homes and businesses. About seven hun-

Campers scattered by hurricane Emily near Frisco, N.C. (Photo courtesy of Drew Wilson/Virginian-Pilot/Carolina Coast)

A crew of Coast Guard workers makes temporary repairs to a house near Buxton after hurricane Emily. (Photo courtesy of Drew Wilson/Virginian-Pilot/ Carolina Coast)

Store owner Ray Couch looks on as workers begin cleanup efforts near Cape Hatteras after hurricane Emily. (Photo courtesy of Drew Wilson/Virginian-Pilot/Carolina Coast)

Emily's destruction was focused on the Outer Banks, where $12.5 million in damages was reported. (Photo courtesy of Drew Wilson/ Virginian-Pilot/Carolina Coast)

dred buildings were badly damaged or destroyed, leaving at least 25 percent of the villages' residents homeless. Damage estimates were near $13 million for the seventeen-mile stretch hardest hit by the storm. Cleanup would take weeks, and in some cases months, as neighbor helped neighbor to rebuild and recover.

As with most every hurricane disaster, volunteers and relief workers poured in to assist in the recovery effort. The American Red Cross, the Salvation Army, the National Guard, and the Southern Baptist Convention offered water, food, shelter, and other assistance. Dozens of state forestry workers removed downed trees and limbs and hauled them away. Utility crews worked to repair electrical lines, broken water pipes, and other services on the island. These agencies and others were quick to respond to the needs of the victims of Emily.

But hundreds of other volunteers also pitched in during the days and weeks following the storm. More than two hundred teachers from Manteo and the northern beaches climbed aboard buses and came to the aid of the devastated school in Buxton. With mops and brooms they scoured the classrooms and offices of the school, enabling classes to begin just two weeks after the flood. Schools across the state held fund-raisers to help with the replacement of equipment and textbooks.

Contractors from around Dare County donated lumber, shingles, and work crews to patch and repair damaged homes and businesses. Church groups arrived the day after the storm with supplies and equipment to help clean and dry out flood-soaked homes. Some residents whose cars were lost to the storm were given loaners by friends on the mainland. Those who suffered most were moved by the generosity of the people who came to their aid. "God bless all of you," exclaimed one elderly Avon resident as workers cleaned her home. "I don't know how we could have managed without your help. Emily may have hurt us but we still have our health and our friends. We're very lucky."

Although no lives were lost on Hatteras Island, Emily delivered the hardest blow to the banks of any hurricane in over thirty years. Businesses were devastated by the storm. Some got back on their feet quickly and displayed crudely painted "open" signs on the plywood that had once boarded their windows. Other businesses took longer to recover but were open in time for the busy fall fishing season. One popular sales item all along the Outer Banks was the now standard T-shirt proclaiming "I Survived Hurricane Emily." Those who actually earned it by enduring the storm wore the message with pride.

NOR'EASTERS

A young boy scrambles to avoid a wave breaking over a high dune in Atlantic Beach during the Storm of the Century in March 1993. (Photo courtesy of Scott Taylor)

The Ash Wednesday Storm of 1962 was as potent as many severe hurricanes. More than eighteen hundred houses were destroyed along the mid-Atlantic coast. (Photo by Aycock Brown; courtesy of the Outer Banks History Center)

Many northeasters have affected the North Carolina coast over the years, causing hurricane-like destruction. A March storm in 1926 flooded Front Street in Beaufort, prompting the evacuation of many waterfront businesses, including the Ramsey Grocery Co. (Photo courtesy of the Carteret County Historical Society)

The press labeled it "The Storm of the Century." Residents along the eastern seaboard called it "the hurricane with snow." But the great storm of March 1993 wasn't a hurricane at all, at least not by definition. It was, instead, a powerful winter storm that meteorologists refer to as an extratropical cyclone. Old-timers will tell you it was just a mean nor'easter.

Extratropical cyclones have many of the same characteristics as hurricanes. Strong counterclockwise winds rotate around an area of low pressure, spreading their destructive energies over thousands of square miles. While over the ocean, these winds pile water along the shore, creating a surge effect that floods low-lying areas and brings extensive beach erosion. They can also deliver heavy rains or, as in the case of the '93 storm, blizzardlike snowfall.

Extratropicals differ from hurricanes in that they lack a central warm-air mass and a well-defined eye. They typically occur during the winter months and may even originate over land. Some begin when a strong low-pressure system in the upper atmosphere transfers its energy to a developing low-pressure system off the mid-Atlantic coast. Others form near the Gulf of Mexico, cross into the South Atlantic, and drift into position off Cape Hatteras. These systems are known as "Hatteras Lows" and have been responsible for billions of dollars in losses along the Atlantic coast over the years.

Northeasters are named, of course, for the ceaseless northeast winds that batter the coast as the storm edges by. And that can sometimes be days, as extratropicals are notorious for stalling offshore while their wind-driven waves

pound the beaches. Erosion is often severe during these winter storms, frequently cutting away at protective dunes and undermining beachfront decks and walkways. Over the years, northeasters have taken a heavy toll on the North Carolina coast, and some have been even more destructive and costly than hurricanes.

The March Superstorm of 1993 was one extreme example of the extratropical phenomenon. This unnamed cyclone carved a deadly path from Cuba, where 3 died, to the Canadian Maritimes, where 4 more lives were lost. The total number of deaths was 238, not including the nearly 50 sailors lost from vessels that sank off Nova Scotia and in the Gulf of Mexico. In all, $1 billion in damage was reported in the United States.

This monster storm was known to most in the east as the Blizzard of '93. It delivered record cold to the Deep South and dumped neck-deep snow from Georgia to Canada. Mount Mitchell, North Carolina, recorded fifty inches, and travel was stalled by the snow in numerous eastern states. The storm's rapid development caught many off guard, even though the National Weather Service had forecasted it almost perfectly. Several hikers were stranded in the Great Smoky Mountains but were later rescued after an extensive search.

In Florida, the storm spawned several tornadoes that wreaked havoc across the state. High winds made deadly projectiles out of debris still on the ground from the aftermath of hurricane Andrew, which had struck the same area the previous summer. In all, forty-four Florida residents were killed in the March storm, surpassed only by the fifty who died in Pennsylvania.

In North Carolina, much of the western half of the state was blanketed by the heavy layer of snow laid down by the storm. Along the coast and through-

When the floodwaters subsided following the Ash Wednesday Storm of 1962, sand was deep in the streets of Nags Head. (Photo by Aycock Brown; courtesy of the Outer Banks History Center)

Strong northeast winds pushed waves across the Outer Banks during the Halloween storm of 1991, flooding portions of Highway 12. (Photo by Drew Wilson; courtesy of the Outer Banks History Center)

Highway 12, the only roadway from Ocracoke to Nags Head, is prone to flooding and washouts during hurricanes and northeasters. (Photo by Drew Wilson; courtesy of the Outer Banks History Center)

Sea foam spattered this Buxton home during a strong northeaster in February 1973. (Photo by Ray Couch; courtesy of the Outer Banks History Center)

A winter northeaster claimed this oceanfront home in Nags Head. Northeasters and hurricanes in recent years have altered the shoreline in the Nags Head area, causing several houses to be lost to the Atlantic. (Photo by Drew Wilson; courtesy of the Outer Banks History Center)

out many eastern counties, gusting winds of hurricane force whipped trees and structures for more than eight hours. In Southport, Wrightsville Beach, Morehead City, and Manteo, sustained winds between 70 and 90 mph were reported, with gusts surpassing 100 mph.

Because of the inland track of the storm, very little precipitation fell along the coast. Winds from the south and west lifted salt spray off the ocean and deposited it on vegetation, power lines, and electrical insulators. As a result, power was disrupted for more than twenty-four hours in many areas, at a time when nighttime temperatures dipped into the twenties. The heavy salt layer "burned" the leaves of trees and shrubs for miles inland. Governor Jim Hunt declared forty North Carolina counties disaster areas in the wake of one of the worst winter storms in years.

One of the most severe northeasters in North Carolina history was the infamous Ash Wednesday Storm of 1962. This intense nonhurricane pounded more than five hundred miles of the mid-Atlantic coast from March 7 to 9. For sixty hours, fierce winds and raging surf battered the Tar Heel coast, especially the northern Outer Banks. The power of the storm and the destruction it left behind cause it to be ranked alongside the worst of North Carolina's hurricanes.

Well-known author David Stick chronicled the disaster in his book *The Ash Wednesday Storm*, which features dozens of photographs by Aycock Brown. Stick detailed the destruction caused by the storm's excessive floods—floods made worse by the alignment of the sun, moon, and earth that created one of the highest lunar tides of the year. Surging ocean waters flattened the protective dune line from Kill Devil Hills to the Virginia border. Near-record storm tides at Cape Hatteras opened an inlet two hundred feet wide just north of Buxton, which was later filled in by the U.S. Army Corps of Engineers.

The Ash Wednesday Storm was more brutal to oceanfront property than many hurricanes. Thousands of homes and cottages were severely damaged, and about eighteen hundred dwellings were destroyed. Total structural damage to the mid-Atlantic states was estimated at $234 million. Although the storm wasn't exactly a typical winter northeaster, it served as a reminder to coastal residents that hurricane-like winds and floods can strike during any season of the year.

CREATURES IN THE STORM

For centuries, hurricanes have lashed the North Carolina coast, battering the people and property of the state. Countless stories have been told of the awesome forces of wind and water and of the harrowing ordeals faced by the victims of these storms. Among these stories of human survival, however, are numerous accounts of how the state's nonhuman creatures survived. Domestic animals and wildlife are, in many ways, just as vulnerable to hurricanes as humans. Their stories have also become part of our fascination with the hurricane phenomenon.

Through the years many isolated portions of the Tar Heel coast have provided haven for feral horses. These hardy creatures have endured blistering summers and barren winters on the thin strips of barrier beach that line the shore, but the ravages of severe hurricanes have thinned their numbers and caused mass die-offs on several occasions. The San Ciriaco hurricane of 1899 drowned hundreds of "banker ponies" as well as scores of cows and goats. So many were reportedly lost that burning their carcasses became the only effective means of eliminating a potential health hazard on the banks.

In the hurricane of 1933, some down-east residents reportedly brought their domestic stock inside their homes as floodwaters approached. Pigs, goats, chickens, and even cows were coaxed up to second-floor rooms to escape the rising tide. Many farm animals were not so fortunate, however. Most of those left to fend for themselves either drowned or were scattered by the storm.

One peculiar story appeared in the *Beaufort News* one week after the storm of '33:

> Down at Roe, which is located on the north end of Cedar Island, some men spied a forty-pound shoat [a young hog] lodged in the crotch of a tree Monday morning after the storm about fifteen feet from the ground. This animal had evidently been carried to this place by the high tide and terrific hurricane wind Friday night. In order to prevent the apparently dead pig from decomposing and causing both stench and disease, it was decided that the animal should be removed and buried.
>
> One of the men climbed the tree with a saw and started to remove one of the limbs of the crotch, so that the shoat would fall to the ground. About the second or third stroke of the saw, the pig came to life and let out an unearthly and demon-like squeal that echoed and reached through the woods around Roe. This unexpected resumption of life on the part of the supposedly dead shoat pretty nearly frightened the rescuer to death. After it dawned on the bewildered men that the pig was really alive, they quickly removed him from the tree crotch.

Well-known "fish-house liar" Rodney Kemp tells that in the late nineteenth century, residents from the island communities of Portsmouth and Diamond City would often flee by boat upon the approach of a severe storm. They

(Page 171)
Wild horses have been longtime residents of several isolated portions of the North Carolina coast. (Photo courtesy of Scott Taylor)

would carry a few possessions with them while they visited friends and relatives on the mainland. Prior to these excursions across the sound it was common practice to gather all the chickens and tie their legs together with twine. The islanders would then place the birds on their backs in the bottom of their boats for the journey to the mainland. Kemp says that the chickens became so familiar with this procedure that they would instinctively jump into the boats with their legs in the air upon the first signs of a storm.

Waterfowl can sometimes become victims of severe hurricanes. Hunters report that ducks seem to "disappear" after these storms, perhaps seeking cover in areas farther inland. In the book *Reflections of the Outer Banks* by Donald and Carol McAdoo, former Corolla postmaster Johnny Austin described the effects of high winds on some waterfowl: "The ducks and geese used to be so plentiful around here that when a storm came up it wouldn't be unusual to pick up $15 or $20 worth that had killed themselves flying into that top wire of the lighthouse. And you only got five or six dollars a barrel for them, depending on the kind they were, so it took a lot to mount up to $15."

As hurricane Donna tracked toward North Carolina in 1960, a large flock of seagulls became trapped inside the storm's eye. Military radar confirmed the presence of the birds, which were carried hundreds of miles northward by the storm. Many of the flock finally escaped near Wilmington when the eye distended to sixty miles in diameter, but hundreds of dead gulls washed up on the beaches between Carolina Beach and Topsail Island in the days following the hurricane.

Hurricane floods often flush out a potential hazard for humans: venomous snakes. During the Sea Islands Hurricane of 1893, numerous deaths were reported from snakebites in South Carolina. Rattlesnakes and cottonmouth moccasins were the likely culprits. In one hurricane, a family was forced to climb onto an oak to avoid the rapidly rising tide, only to find "the branches filled with copperheads and other serpents." Snakes have sometimes escaped the floods by finding refuge in homes and furnishings. After the hurricane of 1876, one Hyde County man found a rattlesnake coiled inside his dresser drawer. The reptile was likely seeking a dry location to ride out the storm.

Many stories have been told of the hurricane's effects on creatures of the sea. After the August hurricane of 1881, the army's chief signal officer for Carteret County wrote in his annual report:

Morehead City, N.C., 24th, over thirty hours in advance of the storm, the skies became blackened with seabirds of every kind, size, color and description, moving rapidly towards the west, as if fleeing from the violence of the coming storm. The strange conduct of the birds was equaled, if not surpassed by the finny tribes, as shown by the latter's rapid flight up Newport River, a narrow, turbid stream. All through the day the fish, in schools of millions, passed up the stream, followed by great droves of porpoise, so thick that the river looked like a slowly moving stream of ink.

27th, birds slowly returning, at Newport, where the stream is very narrow, the fishes and porpoise were so wedged in that they could not move either up or down. The above incident would appear to give evidence of the possession of a wonderful instinct by birds and fishes.

Surging tides sometimes retreat as quickly as they advance. After hurricane Donna passed through Nags Head, "flopping bass and other live fish" were picked up off the streets. After Hazel, a large flounder was found on a sidewalk in Carolina Beach, and blue crabs were seen on the streets of Morehead City. On more than one occasion, the people of Ocracoke have found fish in their furniture, as storm tides washed through their living quarters and deposited marine life all about.

In his book *Ocracokers*, author Alton Ballance relays a story told to him by his grandfather. During the San Ciriaco hurricane, witnesses reported seeing two porpoises swim through the village of Ocracoke when floodwaters inundated the island. For a short time, they became lodged in the forked branches of an oak tree, but rolling waves helped free the pair. They swam away and were last seen crossing the island and entering Pamlico Sound.

Fishermen have been known to land some unusual catches in the days following hurricanes. After the Great Atlantic Hurricane of 1944, large tuna and marlin were reportedly trapped in the surf along the Outer Banks. After hurricane Emily passed by Carteret County in 1993, one fishing pier reported several unusual landings. In addition to a 7-foot, 280-pound bull shark and a silver snapper (normally common to the Gulf Stream), a 27-inch sailfish was caught and released at Sportsman's Pier in Atlantic Beach. "It's been pretty strange," noted one angler. "Emily must have scared all the fish onto the beach."

Powerful hurricanes can be very disruptive to freshwater and marine fish populations. After hurricane Hugo in 1989, large fish kills were reported in the lakes and rivers of North and South Carolina. Most of the kills were the result of lowered oxygen levels in the water, caused by tremendous quantities of leaves, limbs, and other organic matter that flowed into streams and lakes. In some areas, fish kills resulted from wedges of salt water that were pushed upriver by abnormally high tides.

Shellfish populations can be affected by hurricanes as well. North Carolina's harvests of white and brown shrimp have been affected by many storms through the years. Surging tides and excessive rains can prematurely wash shrimp out the inlets and into the ocean. And heavy rainfall can produce bacterial runoff that can force the closing of shellfish waters along the coast. After most hurricanes, the North Carolina Division of Marine Fisheries surveys the impact the storms may have had on commercial species.

Wildlife officials note that although some animals may be affected by a severe hurricane, most manage to endure these storms without harm. According to South Carolina wildlife experts, Hugo offered an extreme test of this theory. Large animals, such as deer, suffered few losses during the storm and actually may have benefited from increased browse created by shrubs and herbs that flourished where trees were knocked down. Entire forests may have been lost, but the animals within them survived fairly well. Experts agree that wildlife can endure a natural disaster like a hurricane far better than they can survive an oil spill or some other man-made catastrophe.

THE NEXT GREAT HURRICANE

When people in North Carolina talk about hurricanes along the coast, they often issue an ominous warning: "We're long overdue for a big one." Certainly, recent storms like Emily, Hugo, and Gloria have left scars across the state and caused millions in damage. But if a truly intense storm like Andrew or Hugo made landfall on the North Carolina coast and moved through the state, the destruction would be much greater than any storm in Tar Heel history.

The extensive development that has taken place along the coast over the last few decades has made North Carolina more vulnerable to hurricanes than ever before. There has been tremendous growth on the Outer Banks, along the rivers and sounds, and on the other barrier islands that line the shore. Tourism has thrived, and more and more people have moved into the coastal region. Dare, Carteret, and New Hanover Counties are three of the fastest-growing counties in the state. They also happen to be three of the most likely to be affected by a major hurricane.

During this period of significant growth, North Carolina has had relatively few hurricane strikes. Those that have affected the state have, for the most part, been minor hurricanes or strong storms that merely brushed by the coast. Hugo's most significant impact on North Carolina occurred far inland, many miles away from the barrier beaches. Consequently, the majority of the state's coastal residents have never experienced the core of a major hurricane. Without that experience, it is possible that some residents have become complacent or developed misconceptions about the nature of a hurricane strike. This could prove to be dangerous should inexperienced residents refuse to evacuate to escape a severe storm.

State emergency planners are well aware of the risks and consequences that a major hurricane could bring to a burgeoning coastal population. Dwayne Moore of the North Carolina Division of Emergency Management knows too well the incredible challenge the state will face when the next big storm rolls through. "If you follow the track of Hazel today, you find a lot of new construction," Moore says. "You have two nuclear power plants that were not there before, you have major military installations, the Port Authority; this is all new since Hazel, so those are extra considerations we have to keep in mind. If we had a hurricane follow the Hazel path, of the same intensity, it would be catastrophic." Moore agrees with those who say that the state is long overdue for a severe hurricane. "North Carolina has been very lucky over the years. Hugo at one time was expected to strike here, but of course it didn't, except for in the inland counties. And one day in the not-too-distant future, we will be hit by an Andrew-type storm," says Moore.

Those who are responsible for hurricane forecasting are also concerned about the threat faced by the people of eastern North Carolina. "Hurricanes certainly haven't gone out of style, that's for sure," says Al Hinn, meteorologist in charge at the National Weather Service office in Wilmington. "As far

The streets of Wrightsville Beach may again be flooded by a severe hurricane, just as they were during hurricane Hazel in 1954. (Photo courtesy of the News and Observer Publishing Co./ N.C. Division of Archives and History)

Through the years, hurricanes have cost our nation many billions of dollars and thousands of lives. Recent hurricanes have caused fewer deaths, but property damages continue to exact a high cost. The next great hurricane to strike the North Carolina coast will likely fit that same pattern. With advance preparation and adequate warning, though, the death toll can be minimized. (Photo by Aycock Brown; courtesy of the Outer Banks History Center)

Hurricanes and northeasters are constantly reshaping the geography of the North Carolina coastline. Structures built on the exposed portions of our barrier islands remain vulnerable to the changes these storms might bring. (Photo by Aycock Brown; courtesy of the Outer Banks History Center)

North Carolina's Outer Banks have some of the most beautiful beaches in the nation, but also some of the most vulnerable to hurricanes and winter storms. (Photo by Drew Wilson; courtesy of the Outer Banks History Center)

as North Carolina is concerned, our threat continues to increase because we are more vulnerable. There are more structures here, and a severe hurricane hasn't struck in recent years. It's been a long, long time since we've had a direct hit from a major hurricane that caused major problems."

Hinn is also concerned about the ever-increasing coastal population and the lead time required for massive evacuations. "The coastal counties have grown by some 20 to 30 percent since the sixties," Hinn says. "What were once summer places are now year-round residences. That's happened at Wrightsville Beach, it's happened at Topsail Island; it's all up and down the Carolina coast."

Emergency planners realize that the evacuation of large summer crowds from the state's barrier beaches may take many hours. Some islands have limited arteries through which thousands of residents and vacationers must exit. Special problems exist at remote locations like Ocracoke, which must be evacuated by ferry. Still, recent storms have tested that state's evacuation procedures, and those efforts have proven successful in removing large numbers of people from harm's way. In fact, the network of communications and procedures that make up North Carolina's hurricane disaster plans are considered somewhat of a model for other states.

Dr. Bob Sheets, former director of the National Hurricane Center in Coral Gables, Florida, recognizes the special problems faced by North Carolina residents. "Indeed, if you look at North Carolina, it is one of the most hurricane vulnerable areas in the country," says Sheets. "Certainly the Outer Banks,

A long line of cars poured off of the Outer Banks in the hours before hurricane Emily struck in 1993. Because access to some North Carolina beaches is limited, evacuation plans must be implemented far in advance of approaching storms. (Photo courtesy of the Coastland Times)

Ocracoke, and right on around through the Wrightsville Beach area—these islands are very vulnerable. These are also statistically some of the more active areas for hurricane strikes. The fact that it takes so long to evacuate these areas makes response to a hurricane extremely difficult."

Sheets wants residents to be aware of the risk: "If you take hurricane Hugo, and you look at the potential for it to strike where it did, it was about a one-in-one-hundred-year event, but it happened. The same thing can take place in the coastal region of North Carolina. Even though a major hurricane like a Hazel or a Hugo is a rather rare event, they happen. No one can tell you if it's going to be this year, or next year, or when. I think people need to be aware that it could happen any year, and at any time during the hurricane season in any year. The fact that you may go ten or twenty years without having a direct impact has no relevance to whether or not you're going to get struck next week."

Forecasters and emergency planners can't predict when we might expect the next great hurricane. The National Hurricane Center does an excellent job of detecting these storms and an ever-improving job of forecasting them, but it has no means to "crystal ball" the weather in the western Atlantic. There is, however, one scientist who may be on the right track toward anticipating trends in hurricane development and intensity.

The U.S. East Coast and the Caribbean may enter a twenty-to-forty-year cycle of intense hurricane activity in the near future, according to William M. Gray, an atmospheric scientist at Colorado State University. Gray's prediction

is based on his studies of rainfall cycles in the Sahel region of west-central Africa. His research has found a distinct correlation between patterns of drought and rain in that region and the frequency and intensity of Atlantic hurricanes.

In the Sahel, droughts lasting twenty to forty years alternate with twenty-to-forty-year periods of abundant rainfall. Since the mid-1960s, this region has been dry, and relatively few major hurricanes have developed. In contrast, a wet cycle through the 1940s and 1950s corresponds with numerous severe storms that battered the Caribbean and the United States. If Gray's theory holds true, the early part of the twenty-first century could bring many intense hurricanes to the shores of North America and the beaches of the Tar Heel state.

Still, no one can say exactly when the North Carolina coast will be hit by the next great storm. Most people generally accept the risk, just as midwesterners accept tornadoes and Californians live with earthquakes. Common sense is

Residents who decline to evacuate for the next great hurricane may face greater consequences than just the loss of electric power. (Photo courtesy of Roy Hardee)

the ultimate weapon against the hurricane threat, and well-prepared coastal residents know that lost property is replaceable — lives lost are lost forever. If a major hurricane threatens, their cars are packed and their plans secured to escape the approaching storm. They know that it's not a question of if — sooner or later *the big one* will come.

HURRICANE SURVIVAL

WHEN A HURRICANE THREATENS

KEEP YOUR RADIO OR TV ON...AND LISTEN TO LATEST WEATHER BUREAU ADVICE TO SAVE YOUR *LIFE* AND POSSESSIONS

North Carolina will again be visited by severe hurricanes. The key to surviving the next great storm will be preparation. The following information is provided as a public service by the North Carolina Division of Emergency Management as a guide for hurricane survival.

BEFORE A HURRICANE THREATENS

Know the elevation of your home above sea level. Get this information from local Emergency Management officials. Your nearest Weather Service office can supply flood-stage data for area streams and waterways. Find out if your home is subject to storm-surge (tidal) flooding.

Know the maximum storm surge that might occur. Information about the potential for inland flooding and storm surge is available through your local Emergency Management office.

Know the route to safety if you have to leave. Plan your escape route early. Check with Emergency Management for low points and the flooding history of your route. Check the number of hours it could take you to evacuate to a safe area during peak evacuation traffic.

Know the location of the nearest official shelter. Emergency Management can give you the location of the shelter nearest your home and explain what you should bring with you. Plan for your family's safety. Know how to contact family members if the need arises.

THE STORM TIDE

MAY BE A HURRICANE'S GREATEST KILLER

TAKE PRECAUTIONARY MEASURES PROMPTLY WHEN THE WEATHER BUREAU ISSUES

HURRICANE WARNINGS

How safe is your home? Near the seashore, plan to relocate during a hurricane emergency. If you live in a mobile home, always plan to relocate.

Inventory your property. A complete inventory of personal property will help in obtaining insurance settlements and/or tax deductions for losses. Inventory checklists can be obtained from your insurance representative. Don't trust your memory. Keep written descriptions and take pictures. Store these and other insurance papers in waterproof containers or in your safety deposit box.

Know what your insurance will cover. Review your insurance policies and your coverage to avoid misunderstandings later. Take advantage of flood insurance. Separate policies are needed for protection against wind and flood damage, something people frequently don't realize until too late.

WHEN A HURRICANE WATCH IS ISSUED

Monitor storm reports on radio and television. If considering moving to a shelter, make arrangements for all pets. Pets are not allowed in shelters. If evacuation has not already been recommended, consider leaving the area early to avoid long hours on limited evacuation routes.

Keep a radio with extra batteries. Your transistor radio will be your most useful information source. Have enough batteries for several days, as there may be no electricity.

Evacuate early! (Photo by Drew Wilson; courtesy of the Outer Banks History Center)

Keep flashlights, candles or lamps, and matches. Store matches in waterproof containers. Have enough lamp fuel for several days, and know how to use and store the fuel safely.

Keep a full tank of gasoline in your car. Never let your vehicle gas tank be less than half-full during hurricane season; fill up as soon as a hurricane watch is posted. Remember: When there is no electricity, gas pumps won't work.

Make sure you have some cash. Remember that automated teller machines also won't work without electricity.

Store nonperishable foods. Store packaged foods that can be prepared without cooking and require no refrigeration. There may be no electricity or gas.

Keep containers for drinking water. Have clean, air-tight containers to store sufficient drinking water for several days. Local water supplies could be interrupted or contaminated.

Store materials to protect your windows. Have shutters, plywood, or lumber on hand to nail over windows and doors. Masking tape may be used on small windows but does not always protect against flying shards.

Keep materials for emergency repairs. Your insurance policy may cover the cost of materials used in temporary repairs, so keep all receipts. These will also be helpful for possible tax deductions.

WHEN A HURRICANE WARNING IS ISSUED

Listen constantly to radio or television. Keep a log of hurricane position, intensity, and expected landfall. Discount rumors. Use your telephone sparingly.

Ocracoke store operators board up their windows in preparation for hurricane Hugo in 1989. Although Hugo made landfall much farther south, the effort to protect their property was worthwhile. Every family and business in the coastal region should develop a hurricane preparation plan. (Photo by Drew Wilson; courtesy of the Outer Banks History Center)

Leave your mobile home immediately. Mobile homes are not safe in hurricane-force winds.

Prepare for high winds. Brace your garage door. Lower antennas. Garbage cans, awnings, loose garden tools, toys, and other loose objects can be deadly missiles. Anchor them securely or bring them indoors.

Cover windows and other large glass. Board up or shutter large windows securely. Tape exposed glass to minimize shattering. Draw drapes across large windows and doors to protect against flying glass if shattering does occur.

Secure your boat. Move boats on trailers close to your house and fill with water to weigh them down. Lash securely to trailer and use tie-downs to anchor the trailer to the ground or house. Check mooring lines of boats in the water, and then leave them.

Store valuables and important papers. Put irreplaceable documents in waterproof containers and store them in the highest possible spot. If you evacuate, be sure to take them with you.

Prepare for storm surge, tornadoes, and floods. These are the worst killers associated with a hurricane. In a tornado warning, seek inside dry shelter below ground level. If outside, move away at right angles to a tornado; if escape is impossible, lie flat in a ditch or low spot. Remember that the surge of ocean water plus flash flooding of streams and rivers due to torrential rains combine to make drowning the greatest cause of hurricane deaths.

Check your survival supplies once again.

IF YOU STAY AT HOME

Stay indoors. Remain in an inside room away from doors and windows. Don't go out in the brief calm during the passage of the eye of the storm. The lull sometimes ends suddenly as winds return from the opposite direction. Winds can increase to 75 mph or more within seconds.

Protect your property. Without taking any unnecessary risks, protect your property from damage. Temporary repairs can reduce your losses.

Keep a continuous communications watch. Keep your radio or television tuned for information from official sources. Unexpected changes can sometimes call for last-minute relocations.

Remain calm. Your ability to meet emergencies will help others.

IF YOU MUST EVACUATE

Know where you are going and leave early.

Be prepared for the shelter. Take blankets or sleeping bags, flashlights, special dietary foods, infant needs, and light-weight folding chairs. Register every person arriving with you at the shelter. Do not take pets, alcoholic beverages, or weapons of any kind to shelters. Be prepared to offer assistance to shelter workers if necessary, and stress to all family members their obligation to keep the shelter clean and sanitary.

Don't travel farther than necessary. Roads may be jammed. Don't let your stranded auto become your coffin. Never attempt to drive through water on a road. Water can be deeper than it appears, and water levels may rise very quickly. Most cars will float dangerously for at least a short while, but they can be swept away in floodwaters. Wade through floodwaters only if the water is not flowing rapidly and only in water no higher than the knees. If a car stalls in floodwaters, get out quickly and move to higher ground.

Lock windows and doors. Turn off your gas, water, and electricity. Check to see that you have done everything to protect your property from damage or loss.

Carry along survival supplies. These should include a first-aid kit, canned or dried provisions, a can opener, spoons, bottled water, warm protective clothing, medications and prescriptions, spare eyeglasses, and a hearing aid with extra batteries, if required.

Keep important papers with you at all times. These should include a driver's license or other identification, insurance policies, property inventories, special medical information, and maps to your destination.

Common sense is the best defense against the threat of a hurricane. Property can be replaced; lives cannot. (Photo courtesy of the Coastland Times)

AFTER THE HURRICANE

If you are evacuated, delay your return until recommended or authorized by local officials.

Beware of outdoor hazards. Watch out for loose or dangling power lines, and report them immediately to local officials. Many lives are lost to electrocution. Walk or drive cautiously, as debris-filled streets are dangerous. Snakes and poisonous insects may be a hazard. Washouts may weaken roads and bridges, which could collapse under vehicle weight.

Guard against spoiled food. Food may spoil if refrigerator power is off for more than a few hours. Freezers will keep foods several days if doors are not opened after power failure, but do not refreeze food once it begins to thaw.

Do not use water until it is safe. Use your emergency water supply or boil water before drinking until you hear official word that the water is safe. Report broken water or sewer lines to the proper authorities.

Take extra precautions to prevent fires. Lower water pressure in city and town water mains and the interruption of other services may make fire fighting extremely difficult after a hurricane.

THE RECOVERY

Insurance representatives will be on the scene quickly after a major disaster to speed up the handling of claims. Notify your insurance agent or broker of any losses, and leave word where you can be contacted.

Take steps to protect property. Make temporary repairs to protect property from further damage or looting. Use only reputable contractors (sometimes in the chaotic days following a disaster, unscrupulous operators will prey on the unsuspecting) — check with the Better Business Bureau. Keep all receipts for materials used.

Be patient. Hardship cases will be settled first by insurance representatives. Don't assume that your settlement will be the same as your neighbor's. Policies differ and storm damage is often erratic.

It takes a team effort. Responsibility for cleanup falls to numerous local, state, and federal agencies. A local disaster coordinator will be on hand to help residents in this effort. For more information, contact your county Emergency Management coordinator.

APPENDIX

HURRICANE	YEAR	CATEGORY	DEATHS
Galveston, Texas	1900	4	6,000+
Lake Okeechobee, Florida	1928	4	1,836
Florida Keys/South Texas	1919	4	600
New England	1938	3	600
Florida Keys	1935	5	408
Audrey (Louisiana, Texas)	1957	4	390
North Carolina to New England	1944	3	390
Grand Isle, Louisiana	1909	4	350
New Orleans, Louisiana	1915	4	275
Galveston, Texas	1915	4	275
Camille (Mississippi, Alabama, Virginia)	1969	5	256
Miami, Florida	1926	4	243
Diane (Northeast U.S.)	1955	1	184
Southeast Florida	1906	2	164
Mississippi, Alabama, Florida	1906	3	134
Agnes (Northeast U.S.)	1972	1	122
Hazel (Carolinas, Northeast U.S.)	1954	4	95
Betsy (Florida, Louisiana)	1965	3	75
Carol (Northeast U.S.)	1954	3	60
Florida, Louisiana, Mississippi	1947	4	51

THE DEADLIEST HURRICANES IN THE UNITED STATES, 1900–1993

Source: NOAA, National Hurricane Center.

Losses from Hurricanes in the Continental United States, by Decades (through 1993)
Source: *NOAA, National Hurricane Center.*

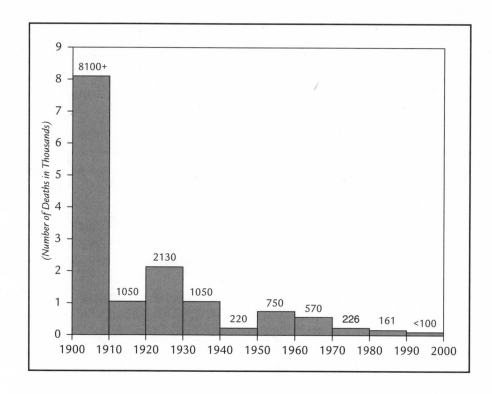

Estimated Losses from Hurricanes in the United States, by Decades (through 1993; damages in 1992 dollars)
Source: *NOAA, National Hurricane Center.*

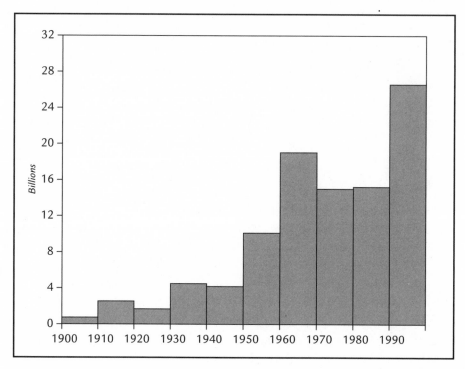

HURRICANE	YEAR	CATEGORY	DAMAGE (IN $ BILLIONS)
Andrew (Florida, Louisiana)	1992	4	25+
Hugo (South Carolina, North Carolina)	1989	4	7.2
Betsy (Florida, Louisiana)	1965	3	6.5
Agnes (Northeast U.S.)	1972	1	6.4
Camille (Mississippi, Alabama, Virginia)	1969	5	5.2
Diane (Northeast U.S.)	1955	1	4.2
New England	1938	3	3.6
Frederic (Alabama, Mississippi)	1979	3	3.5
Alicia (Texas)	1983	3	2.4
Carol (Northeast U.S.)	1954	3	2.4
Carla (Texas)	1961	4	1.9
Donna (Florida, eastern U.S.)	1960	4	1.8
Iniki (Hawaii)	1992	—	1.8
Juan (Louisiana)	1985	1	1.7
Celia (Texas)	1970	3	1.6
Bob (Northeast U.S.)	1991	2	1.5
Hazel (Carolinas, eastern U.S.)	1954	4	1.4
Elena (Mississippi, Alabama, Florida)	1985	3	1.4
Miami, Florida	1926	4	1.3
Galveston, Texas	1915	4	1.2

THE COSTLIEST HURRICANES IN THE UNITED STATES, 1900–1993 (DAMAGES ADJUSTED TO 1990 DOLLARS)

Source: NOAA, National Hurricane Center.

THE MOST INTENSE
HURRICANES IN THE
UNITED STATES AT THE
TIME OF LANDFALL,
1900–1993

HURRICANE	YEAR	CATEGORY	PRESSURE (MILLIBARS)	PRESSURE (INCHES)
Florida Keys	1935	5	892	26.35
Camille (Mississippi)	1969	5	909	26.84
Andrew (Florida)	1992	4	922	27.23
Florida Keys, Texas	1919	4	927	27.37
Lake Okeechobee, Florida	1928	4	929	27.43
Donna (Florida)	1960	4	930	27.46
Galveston, Texas	1900	4	931	27.49
Grand Isle, Louisiana	1909	4	931	27.49
New Orleans, Louisiana	1915	4	931	27.49
Carla (Texas)	1961	4	931	27.49
Hugo (South Carolina)	1989	4	934	27.58
Miami, Florida	1926	4	935	27.61
Hazel (North Carolina)	1954	4	938	27.70
Florida, Mississippi, Alabama	1947	4	940	27.76
Texas	1932	4	941	27.79
Gloria (eastern U.S.)	1985	3	942	27.82
Audrey (Louisiana, Texas)	1957	4*	945	27.91
Galveston, Texas	1915	4*	945	27.91
Celia (Texas)	1970	3	945	27.91
Allen (Texas)	1980	3	945	27.91

*Classified as category 4 because of extreme tides.
Source: NOAA, National Hurricane Center.

NAME/DATE	CATE-GORY	MAXI-MUM WIND	PRESSURE IN N.C. (INCHES)	N.C. DEATHS	N.C. DAMAGE
August 1879	4	168*	na	40+	na
September 1883	3	100+*	na	53	na
August 1899	4	140*	na	25	na
September 1933	3	125*	28.26	21	$3 million
September 1944	3	110*	27.97	1	$1.5 million
Hazel, 1954	4	150*	27.70	19	$136 million
Ione, 1955	3	107	28.00	7	$88 million
Donna, 1960	3@	120*	28.45	8	$25 million
Diana, 1984	3#	115	28.02	3	$85 million
Gloria, 1985	3	100+*	27.82	1	$8 million
Hugo, 1989	3@	100*	28.88	7	$1 billion
Emily, 1993	3	111*	29.00	0	$13 million

SELECTED NOTORIOUS HURRICANES IN NORTH CAROLINA SINCE 1879

*Estimated
@Category 4 elsewhere; at or near category 3 in North Carolina.
#Cape Fear area only, was a category 2 at final landfall.

Hurricane Evacuation Routes. Source: N.C. Division of Emergency Management.

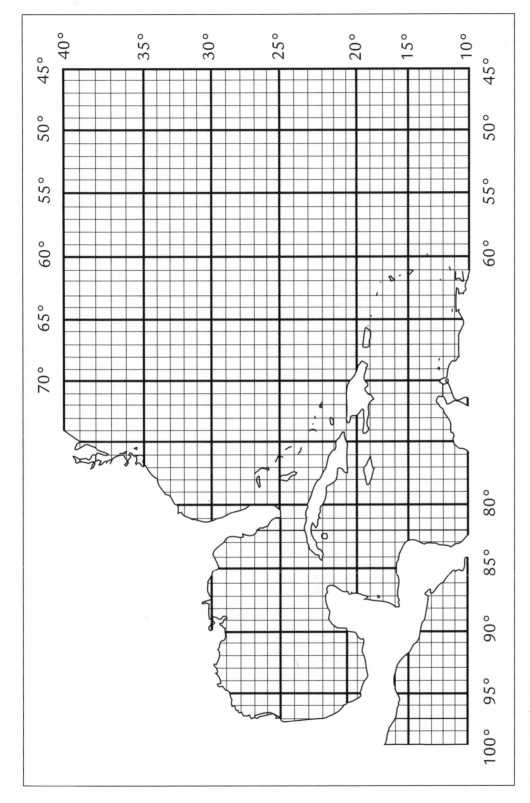

Hurricane Tracking Map

ACKNOWLEDGMENTS

This book was assembled with the outstanding cooperation of many individuals and organizations. Special thanks are offered to those who assisted me in collecting the stories, weather reports, historical data, and photographs. Whenever possible, appropriate credit has been provided for photographic sources.

The primary source of historical and meteorological information used for this text was the National Weather Service Technical Memorandum, *A Historical Account of Tropical Cyclones That Have Impacted North Carolina since 1586*, originally researched by Charles Carney and Albert Hardy and later updated by James Stevenson. This comprehensive publication was used extensively as a resource for details of storm movements, severity, and destruction. Hardy and Carney included numerous uncredited quotations and stories, most of which were borrowed from newspapers and other historical documents. Many of those have been repeated in this book.

Booklets and pamphlets produced by the National Oceanic and Atmospheric Administration (NOAA), the parent organization of the National Weather Service, were the primary resources used in chapters 1, 2, and 3. These excellent publications were useful in providing information on the formation, tracking, and intensity of tropical cyclones.

Chapter 4 relies heavily on the Carney and Hardy publication. Other sources used for this chapter include *Joshua's Dream*, by Susan Carson; a letter from Governor Tryon to Lord Hillsborough from the *Colonial Records, Tryon's Letter Book*; excerpts from the *Raleigh Minerva*; *An Archaeological and Historical Reconnaissance of U.S. Marine Corps Base, Camp Lejeune*, by Thomas Loftfield and Tucker Littleton; and *Graveyard of the Atlantic*, by David Stick.

Weather Bureau records were available for much of chapter 5. Other sources include "An Act of Providence," a widely published article by John Sanders; *The Atlantic Hotel*, by Virginia Doughton; *The Outer Banks* and *Graveyard of the Atlantic*, by David Stick; various articles by Carteret County author Sonny Williamson; reports from the *Raleigh Observer*, the *Beaufort News*, the *Wilmington Messenger*, the *Washington Gazette*, and the *Carteret County News-Times*; and various newspaper reports referenced in articles from the *State* magazine.

Chapter 6 was also compiled with assistance from the Carney and Hardy report, as well as the newspapers mentioned above and the *News and Observer*, the *Greensboro Daily News*, the *Wilmington Morning-Star*, and the *New York Times*; reports from the American Red Cross; letters from the Louis T. Moore Collection at the New Hanover County Public Library; *Sailin' with Grandpa*, by Sonny Williamson; *Ocracokers*, by Alton Ballance; various articles that appeared in *Sea Chest*; "The Great Atlantic Hurricane," an article in the *Hatteras Monitor* by

Rhonda Roughton; "Hurricane Survival on Hatteras," an article in the *State* magazine by Sybil Skakle; several Bill Sharpe articles in the *State*; and *The Hurricane and Its Impact*, by Robert Simpson and Herbert Riehl.

Additional sources used in chapters 7 and 8 include "Hurricane Hazel," an article in the *Tidewater* by Susan Gerdes; *Hurricane Hazel Lashes Coastal Carolinas*, by Wilmington Printing Company, Art Newton, editor; *Making a Difference in North Carolina*, by Ed Rankin and Hugh Morton; various articles from the *State Port Pilot*, the *New Bern Sun-Journal*, the *Coastland Times*, and the *Virginian-Pilot*; an article from the *Duke Power Annual Report of 1989*; the October 1993 issue of the *Hatteras Monitor*; the September 1991 issue of UNC Sea Grant's *Coastwatch*; and personal interviews with Lewis J. Hardee, Tony Seamon, Dorothy Ipock, and other hurricane survivors.

Chapter 9 was developed with the support of several National Weather Service publications on northeasters as well as *The Ash Wednesday Storm*, by David Stick. Sources used in chapter 10 include various reports from the newspapers mentioned above; *Reflections of the Outer Banks*, by Donald and Carol McAdoo; and various Weather Bureau records and reports.

Special recognition and thanks are due to several others who assisted with the completion of this publication. They include Bob Sheets, Al Hinn, and Ed Rappaport of the National Weather Service, Dwayne Moore of the North Carolina Division of Emergency Management, William Gray of Colorado State University, and Spencer Rogers of UNC Sea Grant. Many thanks are offered to those who contributed photographs, especially Jack Goodwin, Roy Hardee, Ed Harper, Hugh Morton, Hellen Shore, Scott Taylor, Drew Wilson, and the late Aycock Brown and Art Newton. Others who deserve special thanks are Cathy Piner, Joe Pelissier of the National Weather Service, my mother, wife, and family, and David Perry and the staff of the University of North Carolina Press.

INDEX

Page numbers in italics refer to illustrations.